Living a Gentle, Passionate Life

Robert J. Wicks

PAULIST PRESS
New York / Mahwah, New Jersey

Other Related Books by Robert J. Wicks
After 50 (Paulist Press)
A Circle of Friends (with Robert M. Hamma) (Ave Maria Press)
Seeds of Sensitivity (Ave Maria Press)
Touching the Holy (Ave Maria Press)
Seeking Perspective (Paulist Press)
Living Simply in an Anxious World (Paulist Press)
Availability (Paulist Press)
Self-Ministry through Self-Understanding (Loyola Press)

Library of Congress Cataloging-in-Publication Data

Wicks, Robert J.
    Living a gentle, passionate life / by Robert J. Wicks.
       p.   cm.
    Includes bibliographical references.
    ISBN 0-8091-0499-7
    1. Conduct of life. 2. Spiritual life. I. Title.
BJ1581.2.W48   1998
158—dc21   98-23205
                                                                CIP

Published by Paulist Press
997 Macarthur Boulevard
Mahwah, New Jersey 07430

Printed and bound in the
United States of America

Contents

→

Contents

Dedication

For those persons whose lives and writings have taught me to live with a little more dignity and a greater sense of wonder and awe:

Abraham Joshua Heschel, Dorothy Day, Robert Coles, Thomas Merton, Martin Luther King, Jr., Mother Teresa, Henri Nouwen, Anthony de Mello, Anthony Bloom, Rainer Maria Rilke and Viktor Frankl.

To them, to my patients, to those with whom I have had the privilege of sharing a mentoring or teaching relationship, and the persons in my family and immediate circle of friends who have called me to go deeper within myself and further out into the world, I offer my gratitude.

They were correct:

> Exchanging comfort for deep peace
> and trading pleasure for real joy
> have always been worth the price!

Acknowledgments

I am grateful to Marie Gipprich, I.H.M., Patricia Mensing, S.S.J., and my editor Maria Maggi for the extensive suggestions they have made. They have helped me to better translate the spirit of my ideas into easy-to-follow, brief "journeys of possibility."

To my wife Michaele, for her overall editorial advice and assistance with the development of reflection questions, I express my deepest feelings of appreciation. For her willingness to interrupt her schedule in response to my frequent requests to "just take a minute to read this bit and tell me what you think," I'm most thankful. I'm sure there is a special place in heaven for a person married to an author.

Finally, to my daughter Michaele, whose periodic "I'm proud of you, Dad" notes help me to remember the importance of having the support of people close to you in life, I say, "You are someone whose goodness is really making a difference in this world; I pray you always know this."

Creating a Gentle, Passionate Life: A Prologue

→

Sometimes dim memories form surprisingly sturdy foundations for the unexpected turns we eventually take in life. As a child, I was fortunate enough to spend each summer on a family farm far away from the noise and crowds of the city. As an adolescent, when these trips stopped, I didn't give them much thought. Yet, now as I walk down a dirt road with those whom I counsel or mentor, I think back to this uncomplicated time in my life. With our sessions interrupted only by the noise of a flock of geese squawking in the distance, I often wonder if those early days spent close to nature were seeding the eventual call for me to live and work in the way I do now.

Shortly after receiving my doctorate in clinical psychology from Hahnemann Medical College, I took what I felt were prudent career steps. I accepted a faculty position at Bryn Mawr College and opened my clinical practice on Rittenhouse Square in Philadelphia. Once I settled into my academic post and clinical work, I also accepted an invitation to join the courtesy staff of a hospital in rural Lancaster County, Pennsylvania. This area is affectionately referred to as "Amish" or "Pennsylvania Dutch" country. For tourists who wish to take nostalgic journeys to see evidence of a yearned-for simplicity still present in today's complex world, it is a peaceful place to visit.

Accepting this part-time position proved to be a small— though ultimately significant— turning point in my professional as well as my personal life. My experiences at the hospital and clinic were to determine how I eventually would envision my own identity as a therapist and, in turn, were to have a major influence on my overall philosophy and spirituality of living. Those years marked the beginning of a deep respect for *simplicity* and *gentleness* that subsequent journeys and attractions could not rob from me.

On Fridays I would drive out to Lancaster from my home in West Chester, Pennsylvania, to interview patients, observe senior colleagues on the ward, and do some psychological testing. Sunday mornings would find me back at the hospital making rounds for the chief psychiatrist. Finally, in midweek I would see patients at a small, rural medical center. (I used to tease that to find this center one only had to drive to the middle of nowhere and then proceed fifty miles further!)

During these early journeys into the country, I plied the psychotherapy skills I had been taught at school. I reflected back what the patients told me without giving them a hint of what I felt. I also remembered to help them become aware of how the past was still being lived out in the present and would ask questions appropriate for this approach, for instance, "Is this feeling that you have a familiar one for you?"

I felt that I was doing all the right things. However, there was a small hitch: nothing positive really seemed to be happening in response to all my efforts. It was no surprise that the patients were generally not happy with the treatment they were receiving, and I was getting frustrated in the process as well.

Finally, after a few months of sensing that little progress was being made, I turned to the psychiatrist who was a mentor for me and shared my concerns with him. Being a generally defensive person, I naturally didn't blame myself for the patients' lack of progress; instead, I creatively projected the fault onto them—quite simply, it was that they were being "resistant" to my sound treatment.

His response quickly cut through my avoidance of the truth. He laughed lightly and said, "Sigmund Freud may have been a wonderful doctor. Yet, I don't think he would have fared any better than you in working with the farm people out here if he had followed the psychoanalytic method. Also, I doubt if after he saw a few cases here, he would continue to use his own general approach. He would realize that a different treatment strategy was necessary. No doubt he then would create a new, more effective one to use with this population."

He motioned me to sit down and relax. Then, after listening to more of my concerns, he offered me the seeds of a basic philosophy of treatment. Over the past twenty years, I have found it not only to be of use in a country setting, but also as a powerful, brief, therapy approach with *all* of my clients. He made me realize that what people under stress in rural areas (and I think just about everywhere else) wanted was not a psychoanalyst or a nondirective counselor. They wanted, instead, an old-fashioned doctor, a "country psychologist," first to hear them out and then to help them work through their difficulties within a reasonable period of time.

In other words, they needed someone who would listen carefully and patiently to their stories, help them analyze their problems and review their talents, take the time to go over the possible treatment strategies available and then provide them with a simple straightforward "prescription." Following these steps, he suggested further that when I saw people for follow-ups, that I review what they had done or had not done, and adjust the psychological—and often spiritual—prescription accordingly so it would have a greater effect on their situation in the future.

As I followed his recommendations, I came to realize that my knowledge of psychodynamics (unconscious forces) and cognitive therapy (helping people see and correct automatic dysfunctional beliefs and inappropriate negative thinking) was also a helpful tool for knowing how best to put his suggestions into practice. The goals I was given were simple: listen, build a doctor-patient relationship, diagnose what you feel is causing the problem, go over the alternatives with the patient, and then provide a remedy—a list of what needs to be done between this visit and the next.

Later, as my experience increased, in the case of difficult long-standing problems (e.g., adult survivors of childhood sexual abuse), I would add the word *patience* in bold letters to my outline. Sometimes it *does* take years to heal certain experiences in life, so the patient—and the doctor!—need to realize this. Also, they often need to be reminded of the value of patience when they get frustrated and feel lost. They will then learn that the wait is truly worth the time invested when both parties are faithful and work hard to gain healthy new perspectives.

Still, this "country psychology"—even though it was to be of great help—wasn't to prove *totally* sufficient for my own life or in my work with others. After a number of years, I reached a point at which I felt that there was still more to learn about working with others as well as about achieving personal insight in my own life. I had a vague feeling of discontent because there seemed to be an important element missing in what I was doing and how I was feeling. I recognized that the simple, yet sound psychology of living that I espoused was only part of the picture. Moreover, I heard similar feelings echoed in the comments of others—including those whom I saw in my city practice—and this made me search further.

My vague discontent eventually led to another crucial turning point for me, and so I sought out a meeting with a different type of mentor—a *spiritual* one. (The specific details of this particular encounter are shared a little later in the book.) This encounter and a review of the writings of the person whom I consulted helped me to appreciate further the real beauty of what we call the "spiritual," "interior" or "inner" life. Not only did this discovery better enable me to see human yearnings from a good psychological vantage point, but it also helped me find what I believe to be a generous source of peace and joy: namely, the strength and warmth that could be found deep within me.

The Inner Life

Most of us are so busy that we never seem to "catch up" in life. Then, at moments of exhaustion, we may fall temporarily into a nostalgia for what we believe was once a more simple past. On the other hand, we might take an opposite tack and launch into worrying about a future that we feel should somehow be more integrated, meaningful and centered.

Much of the time during which we seesaw in this fashion from nostalgia about the past to preoccupation with creating an ideal future, we lament that the most predominant emotions missing in our *present* life are peace and joy. We recognize that on many days we experience vague feelings of alienation, a sense of disconnectedness and a fleeting, wistful desire for a way of life marked by greater clarity, meaning and unperturbable hope.

When these feelings arise on certain days, they encourage us to live more simply and to go more deeply within ourselves. We desperately want to be like persons of great holiness, such as Jesus, or bearers of simplicity and ordinariness, like the Dalai Lama. We also look to emulate people from our own family or circle of friends who have true interior peace, because we want to follow in the footsteps of those who seem—no matter what is going on in their lives—to be in touch with a refreshing sense of inner strength.

In other words, we wish that the thoughts we have about how to live a meaningful and peaceful life would somehow magically sink down from our minds and the realm of desire into our hearts, so that we could begin to live like those we admire. We somehow know that life can be lived more nobly. We have an unspoken yearning for a sense of purpose that will guide our daily lives. We want to live in a gentle, passionate way, now and in the future.

For most of us, however, this sense of what our lives should or could be is often quickly supplanted by a passive sense of resignation to what is. We feel that, for practical reasons, we really have to remain as we are. So, when role models of spiritually alive people come to mind, we become discouraged instead of inspired. We believe that to become like them would be impossible, given our own life's demands. Then, when this feeling of futility becomes pronounced, we give up; melancholy settles in, and the deep desire to search passionately for a more spiritual life that would enable us to live with greater joy and peace fades away.

Instead, we wind up settling for merely chasing periodic pleasure, comfort and security. The search for peace and gentleness is abandoned once again or relegated to a vague corner in our fantasy life until the pressures build up and we return to it once more, only as an "escapist hope." Thus, whereas we read books on solitude, we don't really believe that we have the right or the ability to enjoy healing periods of quiet ourselves. While we admire people who seem to be peaceful and joyful no matter what is going on in their lives, we feel deep within that such serenity will never be our fate.

But does this really have to be? Can we not see this vague sense of discontent and fleeting hope as a call for us to actually live a more spiritual life? Is it so hard to see that trading worry for contentment is worth the journey? Is it so difficult to understand that moving from mere desire to a real commitment to living with God at the center of our lives (rather than just as a Sunday bumper sticker) is not only worth the effort, but is really within our reach?

Once I faced these questions directly and with some sense of commitment and hope, the next natural question for me was: What must I do to move the center of gravity in my own life from competition, greed, anger, worry and overconcern about my image and personal security to a focus on the spiritual life? Or, in religious terms: How do I move God to the center of my life so that I have an attitude that allows me to see everything—both pain and joy—in a way that leads to greater spiritual acuity and a deep desire for holiness?[1] I think that two major components to an overall response to these questions are to listen and to emulate.

Spiritual Listening

Spiritual listening requires that we fashion some quiet time alone. When this period of solitude and silence happens, we can begin to see, maybe for the first time, how loud our inner anxiety and the external negativity and distractions are. When we stop for quiet reflection, we begin to see that one of the major problems we have in listening to the heart of our spiritual self is that the world's anxious noises have drowned out the seemingly little voice of God that speaks of justice, mercy and humility.

Yet, once we make space in silence and solitude, we can then recognize this voice of simple truth—not only when we are alone, but also when we are with others. We are thus able to respond more as people without guile, as ordinary individuals who are able to say "no" when we mean "no" and "yes" when we mean "yes." Our relationships can then have a more "spiritual element." As we listen contemplatively and watch for what is genuine within ourselves, we become more sensitive to what is important and good in others.

When such genuine encounters with ourselves and others are possible, even our suffering in life is altered. It is not that we experience less pain; to expect that is foolish. But with a quiet heart that is able to listen contemplatively without the distractions of external secular values, induced needs and unnecessary internal pressures, greater clarity in life is possible. Accordingly, all things, including—maybe especially—the darkness and pain we experience, can lead to a different type of learning that will offer us new light.

This new light can provide us with the wisdom to convert our ways of viewing life so that our perspective changes radically to the good, and everything is filtered through these lenses of hope. Thus, when worry shows up (as it always will in the human condition), it can be shown to a seat in the back of the theater rather than taking center stage in our life. Since our heart is now the place reserved for spiritual friendship with ourselves, others and God, the door will no longer be left open to a life of unnecessary worry, confusion and fragmentation. To reiterate, it is not that we will experience less pain or fewer problems in our lives; what will change is how we perceive our pain and problems. Life—including suffering—is viewed differently through the lens of simplicity, the clarity of which comes from being spiritually centered and integrated.

Our days are no longer ruined by stress, negative events or disappointments. Unhappy events still bother us to some extent but are not as exaggerated as they were in the past. Instead, since our heart is more centered, we learn from our negative encounters just as we do from our positive ones. The belief that our happiness is determined by outside events rather than our inner life is replaced by a new appreciation for the peace that comes only from within. As Anthony de Mello, Indian psychologist and spiritual writer, once noted in a lecture: The clouds still come in life, but we are no longer the clouds...we are the sky.

Emulation of the Holy

In addition to spiritual listening, emulation of the holy is essential if we are (in Twelve Step language) not simply to think our way into a new way of acting, but also to act our way into a new kind of living! In order to take such actions, though, we must stop seeing holiness as impractical or beyond our reach. Instead, we must look upon our role models of holiness as extra-*ordinary* people and take heart from their lives rather than feeling distanced from them.

We can see this no matter what our spiritual tradition may be. For instance, Gandhi's nonviolent attitude was so simple that it captured the imagination of millions inside and outside of India. His disciples put nonviolence in their hearts and followed this philosophy with their feet as well as with words of protest against injustice. Jesus, in an even more dramatic way, did not cling to his divinity. So, rather than being put off by his Sonship, we can be inspired by his friendship (Jn 15:15); we can see ourselves in him and thus be free to follow his call.

Therefore, the call to be spiritually holy, like the desire to be psychologically integrated, needs to be implemented by a firm decision not to distance ourselves from those we admire who already stand on sacred ground, but to see how we can follow them in our own lives. To do this, we must see such role models neither as threats nor as sources of guilt if we don't measure up. Instead, we need to view them as people on holy ground who are showing us that living spiritually is possible in so many different ways. As a matter of fact, their inspiration should help us to recognize that we, too, occupy that very same sacred ground on which they stand. We need to do this until all of the ground we walk on in our lives (at home, at work and *everywhere*) is seen as holy.

Once, when I was lecturing on the integration of psychology and spirituality, an African student raised his hand and said, "In my country we don't integrate the secular and the sacred." I was surprised by his comment and asked him why this wasn't done. He paused, smiled and softly replied, "Because we never take it apart in the first place."

This is what we must do in seeking to have a sounder, healthier and stronger interior life: we must rejoin the elements in our lives that have been unnecessarily separated. We must blend a spiritual attitude with the practical activities of our day until they are one. In doing this, we will have a sense of inner simplicity and, as Zen masters and spiritual guides are able to do, will begin to see life more purely and honestly, freeing ourselves to act as persons without guile. In other words, we will not just dream about living a gentle, passionate life, but will actually begin creating such a life for ourselves and others right now.

Creating a Gentle, Passionate Life for Yourself

All in all, then, I think the simple philosophy suggested from different vantage points by both of the psychological and spiritual mentors mentioned above has served me well. Now, years later, as I sit in my office in semirural Maryland, on the edge of hundreds of acres of rolling hills and woods filled with waddling woodchucks, flocks of white and green-banded geese and herds of deer, I realize that what I have learned is not only of help to those whom I treat or am asked to mentor, but is also of great service to me as I live out the remainder of my own life. In formulating a basic approach to encourage others, I have also been able to carve out a simple, gentle way of living and seeing the world for myself.

As I walk with others through the fields while I listen to their difficulties or questions, and take similar journeys myself through the woods in order to enjoy some quiet time during my breaks, the little lessons and stories concerning what really matters in life come back to me. Again and again, I see some major mistakes repeated in our daily interactions. In response, I seek the words and actions that tend to bring us back to the refreshing center of our being so that we don't drift too far off our course— the pursuit of a hopeful and meaningful life.

The following pages contain some of these basic spiritual and psychological principles. In addition, I offer the stories I favor most when illustrating points for others as well as when I need to recall them for myself. I share them with you here with the knowledge that while they are simple (as in the case of all good lessons in life), they are unfortunately sometimes not as easy to follow as we'd like because of our resistance to change.

Shortly before his death, Anthony de Mello, to whom I referred earlier, jokingly threatened to write a book entitled *I'm a Fool...You're a Fool* (though he used slightly "stronger" language than "fool"). I think that he said this because he knew how we can tie ourselves up in psychological and spiritual knots—even while we are simultaneously swimming in a sea of potential joy and peace. What he recognized was this: Knowing the truth about living well is one thing; practicing it effectively is obviously quite another!

Still, I think that when we hold onto the easy-to-remember stories in this book, then the simple, hopeful way of living they can nourish will grow deep within us and slowly alter both our attitude and our behavior in positive ways. In essence, they can gently educate our hearts. Good stories truly can do this!

I obviously believe that positive change is possible. As a matter of fact, I think that it is *essential* if we are to meet the new challenges and rewards that each day brings. One thing my walks through the seasons of people's lives (including my own) have taught me is this: Nature punishes without mercy an unwillingness to change when it is necessary to do so.

Still, the good news is that when the right lessons are learned and absorbed into our attitude of living, change *is* possible; creating a gentle, passionate and more spiritual life is possible. Moreover, when we do change positively, we find ourselves living in a fashion that allows us to be more creative and less defensive, more joyful and less needy, more honest and less grasping. We see, in fact, that all of the efforts we undertake to remember and practice little lessons in meaningful living are indeed well worth the work—not only for us, but also for those who look to us for encouragement and guidance. Thus, my hope for you is that the following stories and ideas about living peacefully and simply in today's complex world will support you as they have continued to nourish me, so that we can take this journey together to find the new life that is already there before us, if only we take the next step.

Robert J. Wicks
Loyola College in Maryland

A Note to the Reader

→

At the end of each chapter ideas, themes or questions will be presented for reflection. This book was written in the hope that the reader will read the material over a longer period of time than is usual for a book of this length. The reflection questions following each chapter ideally should be considered or even pondered over for a few days to allow the ideas and stories to take seed in one's heart.

To do this, I would suggest writing down the reflection questions on a piece of paper or an index card and then sitting with them for a few minutes in silence and solitude each morning. It would also be beneficial to look back at the questions several times during the day and to think about them again before retiring for the night.

Another option would be to write down one's thoughts with respect to the reflective themes in a little spiral notebook. When this is done over a period of a couple of days to a week, the reader will see how the principle has been made one's own through the processing of personal experiences and ideas.

As we progress, resistances to change will also surface. In praying over the simple tenets of meaningful living we will come up with a whole myriad of reasons why these principles will not work in our lives. That's fine. It's normal. The key is to accept these resistances without totally believing them or condemning oneself for not wanting or being able to change. All of us can change for the better. We just need to make friends with our resistance to change by recognizing our hesitation, taking small steps to change and laughing at ourselves when we undermine the seeding of simple principles of spiritual and psychological health deep within ourselves.

1. Single-Heartedness and Simplicity: Sources of a Healthy Perspective in Life

→

Perspective, the way we view ourselves and life, is one of the most dramatic causes of a person's joy or depression. We may be vibrantly passionate toward the day, or feel depleted by the demands of the future long before it unfolds, depending on our attitude toward life. Thus, we must take great care to uncover what may unconsciously be contributing to our perspective on things.

To appreciate the important role attitude and perspective play, we need only look around us. Examples of how important our attitude is in determining our views of events abound in life.

For instance, ten years ago I was sitting with an older colleague in one of my favorite places, a country diner. Roadside diners lure in truckers for large meals and attract people like myself for thick slices of rich pie and wonderfully tasting coffee. They are great spots to sit, chat...and get fat!

We were doing just that when my companion, also a psychologist, startled me with a claim about herself that I felt couldn't possibly be true. She had been expressing a concern about her own ability to be empathic with people in pain.

I was quickly engrossed in her story for a very simple reason: of all the psychotherapists, mentors and guides I have met over the years, Beth clearly was one of the most patient and kind. As proof of her perceived shortcomings, she went on to note the comments a few of her counselees had made to her over the past six months. She said in a quiet voice, "They said that I was a lovely person, but I couldn't understand what they were going through because life had been so easy for me."

I was about to interrupt her in order to point out that all of us have had that reaction from persons going through great emotional pain and spiritual hunger. She quickly added, however, before I had a chance to say anything, "You know, I think they are right. I *have* had an easy and wonderful life."

Finally, she paused for a moment, and I took the opportunity to intervene. With a voice full of doubt and irony I said, "*You* have had a wonderful life?" Implicit in my question was my knowledge of her background. Her only son had had major problems all through high school, and her husband had been battling problems resulting from chronic unemployment for years. She had also been crippled as a child. Only through painstaking effort— by pulling herself up along a picket fence as a way of forcing herself to stand and move — had she eventually been able to walk.

I went on to add, "No, Beth. You haven't had an easy life. Your secret is that *you have learned to take your own life easily*. You have an attitude that has helped you be deeply grateful and open to life. From the gray and dark periods of your life you have learned how to avoid the terrible danger of 'entitlement.' Suffering didn't make you bitter. Instead, it reminded you not to take life's daily little gifts (like your morning coffee or an afternoon walk with your son) for granted. Achieving and maintaining a healthy perspective in both good and bad times is possible for you because of this ability. If your life has been good, it is because of this and not because pain and defeat have been absent from your experience. I only wish my attitude was as spiritually and psychologically healthy as yours is."

To return us to the context of psychotherapy, I then added what we all must be reminded of as helpers: "You know that once your patients reach a certain point in the therapy, in some way they will have a good chance to absorb what you model and live. The recovering alcoholics, survivors of abuse and those who have experienced the death of a child in their lives will eventually take courage from your relationship with them.

"They will not equate themselves with their pain but will learn from it instead. Their pain will not freeze in bitterness if they give you and the therapy a chance. Instead, it will form the basis for a solid, new psychology and spirituality that are more real than the ones they brought with them into therapy. They, in turn, will be gifts of compassion for others who, like them, are battling alcoholism, the results of abuse or the painful and hollow feeling within that results from the loss of a loved one."

Over the next several months, I thought a lot about that conversation. Beth has a key to life that many of us lack most of the time. It is a sense of perspective that comes from having such a wonderful attitude toward life. Even when she is facing hard times, she makes it look so easy that people think she hasn't been challenged by difficult circumstances. At some level, I and others yearn to be like her but know this isn't as easy as it looks.

Knowing that a psychologically and spiritually healthy attitude is desirable and necessary for deep inner peace is one thing. Having the ability to seed such an attitude in our own hearts on a day-to-day basis like Beth does is obviously yet another. So, unfortunately, although a good attitude is something we often speak about, in reality, it is truly a rarity because we don't consciously take the necessary steps to achieve a healthy outlook grounded in gratefulness.

One French priest who had heard the confessions of others for many years was asked once if he had learned anything from being present to others. He paused, nodded his head yes, and said rather sadly, "People are not very happy and we never grow up."[2] I don't think he was exaggerating.

From a psychological perspective, one therapist observed that this same sentiment was even dominant in those people who came to him seeking to change themselves for the better. He said, "Every patient stared at long enough, listened to hard enough, yields up a child, arrived at from somewhere else, caught up in a confused life, trying to do the right thing, whatever that might be, and doing the wrong thing instead."[3] Or, in the famous words of Paul the apostle, "I do not understand my own actions. For I do not do what I want but I do the very thing I hate" (Rom 7:15).

Thus, even those of us who wish to view the world with gratitude, awe and a healthy sense of perspective need some direction if we are to overcome the natural obstacles we encounter. We need a way of viewing ourselves and the world that truly allows us to appreciate all the wonder that is in and around us and keeps us from being overwhelmed by the negative in life. Memorizing a lot of techniques is not what changes us; rather, it is in having *the right attitude*– one that will offer us the information or angle of vision that we need when the time comes for us to respond to pain and negativity.

Zen experts put it this way: Face reality and unwilled change will take place. Jesus put it another way: "Do not worry about how you are to speak or what you are to say; for what you are to say will be given to you at that time" (Mt 10:19). In other words, to use yet another scriptural metaphor: "If your eye is healthy, your whole body will be full of light" (Mt 6:22). Perspective as an outgrowth of a healthy psychological and spiritual attitude is truly what matters! When we view ourselves, others and the world properly, then all we look at finds its proper place. Since whatever we can do to seed such an attitude is worthy of our attention, much of what follows will address this need in some way.

Sources of a Healthy Perspective in Life

Single-Heartedness, Effort, and Sensitivity

A healthy spiritual and psychological attitude that helps us gain and maintain a wholesome perspective is steeped in an appreciation of the value of *single-heartedness*. It also involves a sincere willingness to seek what is important in life and a special sensitivity to those existential elements of our being that help us to discern what is truly at the heart of our limited time on this earth. Of these three elements, however, *single-heartedness* is the most essential.

In 1997 I attended a conference in Corpus Christi, Texas. Although I had been a long-term member of the organization hosting it, I hadn't gone to one of the meetings for many years. As a result, I knew very few of the people. That was fine for the most part since I enjoy solitude; even dining alone can be quite relaxing for me. However, after a couple of days I yearned for a friendly face.

Finally, I met a former counseling student of mine who was a few years younger than I. I had always liked and respected him. As both pastoral counselor and priest, he had a true healing presence that manifested itself in both his therapeutic work and his ministry.

After chatting with him for a few minutes, I asked if he were free for dinner. He was, and we made plans to go off into town later that evening. The restaurant turned out to be one with good food and a relaxed atmosphere, so we had a chance for a leisurely dinner and stimulating conversation.

About halfway through our meal, he surprised me, though, with the comment: "Something you mentioned in class several years back has always stuck with me. As a matter of fact, I have mentioned it to a number of people."

"What was it?" I asked with a good deal of curiosity.

He said, "You told us that if we wanted peace, we could have it—as long as that was all we wanted!"

I am glad that he remembered this comment and valued it as I did. Single-heartedness is embracing the pearl of great price (in this case a spiritually pure and psychologically healthy attitude) so that we can enjoy the other jewels of life in their proper places. Single-heartedness cultivates the proper perspective with which to see the wonderfully graced elements of our life and appreciate their beauty without being dominated by them.

This becomes possible to a greater degree when we are willing to exert the effort to view life through the prism of an attitude that enables us to appreciate mature values and discern what is truly important. This helps us to avoid following the crowd in its search for comfort, security, power, success and control; it enables us to have an appreciation of what peace and joy can offer. However, as in the case of any insight of great worth, the simplicity of the concept often cloaks the fact that "simple" does not equal "easy."

Effort

The existential philosopher Sartre's comment that "To live well is both difficult and possible"[4] has never left me. A life of simplicity and peace, an attitude of deep gratefulness is possible, but it takes effort, which is something that most of us don't want to exert.

One morning as I walked around a lake with a patient of mine, I remember her saying to me that she felt that she was out of step with others. She said, "I'm working the Twelve-Step Program in A.A., I'm in therapy and yet I wonder about so many others who don't seem to be putting the effort out that I am. I also see their different values and the worries that come along with them and think: Am I crazy or are they? I hope I don't sound too dramatic or self-righteous, but that's what I'm grappling with now."

In our discussions, she finally came to the recognition that 95 percent of the people in the world are satisfied with merely existing, tolerating some pain and experiencing some highs. Very few want to expend the energy *to really live*. They feel that it is either out of the question for them or, as in the case of no-effort diets, should be as easy as saying mantras of positive words. The reality about a well-lived life, however, is that it is both difficult and possible. This is why it seems very lonely when we are trying to travel the path to a more psychologically healthy and spiritually centered life.

During a therapy session with a very talented psychologist who was looking for greater self-awareness and growth, I made an interpretation designed to summarize her comments. My hope was to increase clarity concerning the different levels of motivation that she seemed to have regarding the actions she had just taken. Instead of pondering my reflection, immediately after I finished speaking she looked straight at me and blurted out with a laugh, "The problem with you is you expect entirely too much health!!"

Although she made the statement jokingly, she actually was right about me. I do expect a great deal of health from myself and from anyone else who comes to see me professing the desire to live a gentle, passionate life. There's just no way around it. A meaningful life takes effort to achieve.

Sensitivity to the Now

As was just mentioned, psychological health requires some work on our part— as does living a richly spiritual life. However, not just any effort will do. Instead, it is essential for us to embrace the following:

Be sensitive to the moment in which we are now by having a true awareness of the reality of the limited time we have at our disposal.

Be aware of the current things or people we are actually worshiping (instead of simply enjoying) in our lives now.

Have an appreciation of the essential interplay between psycho-spiritual development and compassion in our lives.

The present moment is something very precious. It is a fleeting moment of grace we need to value, for there will never be another one like it. The problem is that we often don't appreciate the *now* while it is before us. We think about it only later when the true energy of being in the moment is gone. Thus, to appreciate the *now* we must take responsibility for attending to it and acknowledging our role in the loss of the experience if we do not achieve full awareness.

I went to spend a week in Fort Myers with some friends a few years back. One evening we visited the island of Captiva, where we planned to have dinner and then watch the sunset. When we arrived for dinner, we asked for a table by the window. The hostess responded to our request by saying, "No problem." She then proceeded to lead us to a table in a windowless corner. After we were seated and received the menus, I said to her, "I thought you were going to sit us by the window?"

"Oh, that's right," she said. "Wait a minute. I'll take care of it." She left and came back, rolling to our table a short wall with a window in it. She placed it by our table, and said, "There you go—a table by the window!" (Everybody is a comedian today!)

Finally, after having a very enjoyable dinner sparked in part by the joke the hostess played on me, we scooted across the street to the beach to get a good spot on a large rock to watch the sun melt into the ocean. The sunset was magnificent. Rich colors streamed out from both the sky and the ocean, spurring deep feelings within me. I was awed—not just with the sunset but with my life at that very moment.

Then, just after the sun, a young fellow and his girlfriend ran onto the beach. Obviously disappointed that they had missed the sunset, the young man said in an almost whiny voice to friends who had been sitting on a rock, "I lost track of time because I got a phone call." The implication was clear: "It's not my fault I missed it." To this, his friend replied, "Too bad, man."

Yet, I think that if "nature" could also respond to this young man at this point, it would have advised him with these words: "It doesn't matter whose fault it is. It doesn't matter whether you are good or bad, whether you are doing something worthwhile or not. The bottom line is this: If you're late for a sunset, you miss it. Case closed." Or, in the words of a famous Chinese proverb:

In nature there are no rewards and punishments...just consequences.

The *now* is a simple gift that either we are there to receive or we are not. Excuses, no matter how good, unfortunately can't change that. In our lives we have only so much time to appreciate what is before us. If we miss it, so be it.

Too often the reason we do miss the wonder of the *now* is that we are preoccupied with the past or the future. Maybe what would help us avoid spending our time inside the silver casket of nostalgia or continually preoccupied with what lies ahead would be a simple, stark awareness of our own limitedness, our impending death some time in the future.

Still, when the subject of death surfaces, people react in one of three ways: they deny their own mortality, claim one is being morbid by talking about such things or feel the practical thing to do in life is to prepare for the future as if it were endless. A story might help here to emphasize the preciousness and the limited nature of our lives. When I heard it the first time, it woke me up and I have never forgotten it. The story goes like this:

A man who had a very thriving business prepared well for his own financial retirement. He even prepared to the point that he planned a year of reflection after his retirement in which he would decide on how to spend his days fruitfully as well as to decide on how to invest his sizable funds.

However, in the first month of retired life, he was diagnosed with a fast-moving cancer. After denial, anger, deep sadness and resentment at this bad turn of luck, he did some journaling. Before he died, the following line stood out as a warning on one of the pages: "If you have enough health and money to live, then live. Don't save up to the extent that you miss what is present in front of you now in the misguided hope of controlling a beautiful future that you may never see. At least die being alive!"

Is this thinking on his part considered to be impractical for those of us who have not yet been diagnosed with a quick-moving terminal illness? Obviously not. Instead it is a wake-up call we can choose either to hear or dismiss. But again: IT IS UP TO US.

Who or What Are You Worshiping?

The man in the previous story worshiped his future until it was too late. He spent all of his energy planning for what he felt would be the best time of his life. This is a potential danger for all of us. Anytime we worship something less than the Truth (what some of us would call a spiritual awareness of the living God), we deplete our lives of energy and prevent simplicity and single-heartedness from taking root. We cease to see the beautiful value in being ordinary.

It is easy to find out what it is that we worship so that we don't have to wait until we are ready to die to see the truth. And, once again, we can rely on the words of Jesus for guidance. When we are faced with the temptation toward duplicity or burdened under the stress of being pulled in many different directions, we must remember that he said, "Where your treasure is your heart is" (Mt 6:21).

In saying this, he was pointing out to those he was teaching (including us today) that you can't serve two masters. Either we see life through one lens or we become confused and torn in many different directions. Jesus also warns that the quality of our lives will be effected if we make our decisions based on that which we recognize as spiritually inferior. While this can produce sporadic comfort, success and power, it fails to afford us a deep sense of abiding peace and joy. It is as simple and as terrible as that.

24

A good way to find out what it is that we worship is to see what elicits the most emotion in us. What troubles or preoccupies our mind so that we are unable to enjoy each day before us? Is it not getting our way? Being insulted by another? Losing power or control over our image? Or is it feeling insecure or not getting the closure we seek on things? Again, what is it that prevents us from being fully alive? In essence, on what are we anxiously pawning away our single-heartedness on?

To be sure, it might be something "good." Maybe it is the welfare of our children or our success at work. Maybe it is our desire to accomplish something meaningful— even good goals can be the most dangerous of idols because they can easily slip from being activities that are worthwhile to being gods in themselves. Also, I think we erroneously fear that if we are single-hearted— have a healthy attitude at the core of our being— we will in some way lose our connections with what we presently enjoy and love in life. Nothing could be farther from the truth. Single-heartedness actually helps us to enjoy life *more* because we are able to appreciate everything in our world without being captured by it. Also we don't waste energy trying to grasp and control what is good in life; likewise, we don't erroneously seek to be "terrorists of the soul," rejecting all of creation's gifts in a misguided form of extreme asceticism designed to combat our unhealthy attachments and greed.

What can help us monitor this tendency toward loss of perspective, though, is to seek to keep our connection between spirituality and compassion unbroken so that our life doesn't risk imbalance as we seek for that which is good. It is true that by focusing on *both* our own spirituality and the welfare of others, everything in life worth enjoying can be welcomed without our forsaking the welfare of our own souls or the care of others we meet in life.

The Circle of Grace...
Spirituality and Compassion

The development of our own inner life and our reaching out to others are intertwined. They make up a circle that surrounds and feeds both our own spiritual selves and those with whom we interact during our lifetime. If this "circle of grace" is broken and spirituality is divided from compassion, two dangerous extremes may result.

One is that spirituality may develop into a narrow form of piety called "quietism." We will withdraw from the world and, instead of finding time with God, we will simply be alone with our own ego. Security and comfort will become our obsession, and the perspective that can be brought to us by our interaction with others will be lost. We need compassion for others to help center us and to bring out the love that is within us so that it doesn't wilt or lie dormant. On the other hand, when we seek to be compassionate without time for prayer and quiet reflection, our reaching out runs the risk of degenerating into compulsive forms of giving that may be lavish but not very genuine.

Thus, the circle of grace is simultaneously the basis and fruit of a gentle, passionate life. It feeds single-heartedness and challenges it. It also helps us to keep perspective so that we don't inordinately pull back from life or in some way forsake taking care of ourselves so that we wind up burned out and discouraged. Therefore, to keep the circle intact, we must attend to both quiet reflection on the one hand and active sharing with others on the other, so that our life remains balanced, alive and filled with fresh energy, wisdom and *self-respect*– an important aspect of the journey toward a gentle, compassionate life.

· · · · · · · ·

FOR REFLECTION...

Idols need not be made of stone or gold; they need only be substantial enough to serve as "stumbling blocks" in the path toward holiness. Are you able to recognize your own (occasional or persistent) attitudes that stand between you and God? What holds you back from living more fully in God's image?

How is the "circle of grace" (the interaction and balance of prayer and compassion) operative in your life?

2. The Music of Gentle Self-Respect

→

Occasionally we receive feedback that simply and powerfully helps us to see something that we have missed although it is at the heart of life. It helps us to recall these moments of epiphany because they are mustard seeds of spiritual wisdom that grow within us. If they are carefully and gently nourished through reflection, journaling and discussion with good friends and mentors, they add depth and strength to our inner lives.

As a way of illustrating this, I would like to share a special experience. It started with my asking a simple question and ended with an insight that I have recalled again and again in my writings and lectures. It helps me to remember an elementary lesson of life that can be easily forgotten.

The time was late fall. Most of the leaves were gone and the landscape around my office was burnished in brown. The air still felt some of summer's warmth, and we were still several weeks from the time when the scenery surrounding the usual route I walk with my patients would turn into a dull winter gray. The sky was a pure, deep blue. It was just cool enough for wearing a light sweater and yet warm enough to remember the last days of summer.

As I stepped outside with a person who had been seeing me professionally for a number of years, I felt that both she and I were in good places in our lives. We walked on a path cut by tractors through the tall grass in the fields that serviced a pipeline that quietly traveled unseen through an underground section of the grounds.

We were at the end of a long-term therapy. The patient had been sexually abused as a child and had made amazing strides in therapy as an adult. I had watched as her confidence grew; her sense of self became enthusiastically positive, letting her creativity flow freely and energetically.

About halfway through our walk, she seemed filled with great energy. And, as I watched and listened to her, I thought it might be a good time to help her to appreciate how far she had come. I also thought that if I intervened at this point I might be able to get her to take more credit for all of the fine work she had done in therapy. This would help her to know how to apply her insights in the future, when dark times would come again, as they do for us all from time to time.

So, I stopped on the path, looked at her, and said, "Let's stop for a moment. I have a couple of questions."

She was in the middle of a story, so she was a bit surprised but did as I asked and responded, "What are they?"

"Picture my eyes as a mirror. As you look at them, what do you see?"

She smiled radiantly, showing that she would enjoy this exercise, and said, "I see a person filled with great life. Someone who is excited that she is finally able to find the joyous little girl in herself who had been there before but was lost due to abuse. She has now combined that child with the full grown woman she is now." Then, after a pause, she added with a big smile, "*And,* she is thoroughly happy about it all!"

"Yes." I told her. "That's what I see, too. Given this, the second question I have for you is how did you get to this point? When you first came to see me, you weren't in this place."

My expectation was that she would provide a fairly detailed review of the concrete steps that she took to change her way of viewing herself and the world. Instead, she made a half frown, looked straight at me with her dark brown eyes and said, "You mean you really don't know?"

Taken a bit off guard, I responded, "No. I really don't exactly know."

"Well, it was easy." she said.

> *When I first came in to see you,*
> *I simply watched the way you sat with me.*
> *Then I began sitting with myself in the same way.*

For a while I was silent. I had forgotten how a respectful presence to others could be so truly transformative. Such a gentle way of being with others opens up possibilities that are not there when they are able to view themselves only in narrow, unnecessarily negative and distorted ways.

When we respect others and help them question their own and others' past and present views of themselves, we can help them break through the long-held erroneous beliefs that have been the driving force behind poor self-esteem and destructive or inappropriate behavior. Change is possible in such situations because when one's views and experiences of self are altered, one's central attitude can change as well. An additional example might help here.

About ten years ago I had treated another survivor of sexual abuse. (The high percentage of persons abused as children that you often read about is unfortunately accurate. It is amazing how many adults today were abused when they were young. I don't think that the numbers have increased from days gone by. I think this terrible reality is just finally coming to light and being addressed.) She had a very negative view of herself and was acting out negatively in so many ways. After several sessions, I picked up the very poor view she had of herself and I commented on it. "You seem to see yourself in such a terribly negative light. On what do you base this?"

She stuck out her chin a bit and said, "I have plenty of proof that I am not worth much. I'd like to give myself a lot of positive messages, but then I see the reality of my life." (She was only eighteen years of age and sounded like life had already passed her by.) "I have gotten drunk and passed out. I've been involved with all kinds of men. I have been angry, explosive, wasted my time in school and broken my mother's heart time and time again—and, as a single parent, she certainly didn't need grief from me."

My response caught her off guard. "I'm afraid that proves nothing. You could continue along those lines with more examples and it still wouldn't prove you are worthless as a person. But it does indeed prove something else about which you need to be aware."

Her facial expression showed that she was more than intrigued (though still somewhat doubtful) about what I would say and, almost in spite of herself, wanted me to continue. "What does it prove then?"

I went on to explain to her that when she was sexually abused as a child, it wasn't her fault. She didn't do anything wrong. She was innocent then, as she is innocent now. The key was the long-held belief in her heart that somehow it was her fault, that something was wrong with her. As a result, this vague but powerfully depressing music played within her, and she looked for lyrics to fit the music. In other words, she acted out in ways that fit her belief. Yet, it remained that she was not the person she believed she was, and all the negative actions in the world would not prove it. The only thing such actions could do was to perpetuate in her mind a self-image that was false.

In subsequent therapy sessions, I began to focus on helping this young woman to recognize her false sense of self. This deep negative belief (what I refer to as our "music" or the self-imposed rumors we believe about ourselves) needs to be surfaced so that it can be confronted. It is important to assertively stand against that which has been negatively programmed into ourselves so that we can restore natural self-respect.

Altering one's sense of self takes time. Even those of us who have not been sexually abused are still loyal to many negative perceptions about ourselves that were learned early in life. Therefore, we need to surface old roles and views of us that parents, brothers, sisters and childhood friends assigned to us.

The issue at hand is that we need to recognize that those people who knew us as children were reacting only to part of us. They didn't know what or who we would be as adults. They also acted out of their own needs and deficits. No one person— no matter how well meaning— can truly capture or reflect all of our goodness in attempting to understand us as human beings. Even people who love and respect us can't view us totally. Who we are is an ongoing process, both psychological and spiritual.

Thus, we must be sensitive to ourselves, find a sense of identity that fits us *now*, and then act out of that sense of self. The words that may help us to reflect on these three processes which lead to greater and more gentle self-respect are *listening, finding* and *being.*

Listening

The paradox is evident. People speak about the value of listening, but few really value it enough to expend energy in this area— this includes people like myself, who are supposed to be professional listeners! I learned the curative value of listening from one of my own patients soon after I had graduated from Hahnemann Medical College and opened my own clinical practice in psychology.

The call came in at a break in the midafternoon. "Dr. Wicks, I really need to see you. Tonight, if possible."

"Is it an emergency?" I asked.

"No. Not really. But I do want to share something now. I think that it is important."

"Well, if we can postpone it, I would be able to give you a better hearing during your next regularly scheduled appointment. I've been seeing people since early morning and the only opening would be at the end of the night at 9:00 P.M."

"Oh, that would be fine. I'll take the 9:00 P.M. slot."

"Are you sure?"

"Absolutely! See you then."

After I hung up the phone, I was a bit sorry that he decided to come. I was tired already and felt that I wouldn't be much use to him. Beyond this, though, my pride was somewhat at stake. In the past several months, I had made what I felt were some very good interpretations and interventions. I felt that this session wouldn't meet the same standards, and that my patient would be disappointed.

To make the situation worse, when he did come in, I was even more tired than I thought I would be. However, I had agreed to see him, so I needed to go on with the session. After he greeted me and sat down, he immediately launched into the story he wished to tell me. I must confess, as I listened to what he shared, I couldn't think of even one intelligent comment to make. Not only wasn't I as "brilliant" as I felt I was in the past, but I didn't even make the usual audible sounds of encouragement. Finally, after seeing by my watch that forty-five minutes had passed, I looked at him and said, "Well, I see that our time is up for this evening."

He responded by saying, "Oh, yes, so it is." Following a few additional comments, he got up, thanked me profusely for seeing him at so late an hour and headed for the door. But, at the last minute, he turned around and said, "You know, I think that this is the *best* session we have ever had!"

In return, I stared at him silently, wide-eyed, and thought to myself, "I feel like bopping him right on the head."

I don't think that any of us fully realizes how being listened to is so very, very important. More and more, I have learned that attentively *being* with someone is essential for the person's health and growth. In order to develop, we need to be heard by others, to share our life story, feelings, ideas, fears and hopes. That is why speaking with a friend or family member in the evening about the little activities of our day is so healing— even if we do it over the phone or by writing a note. In a similar vein, this is also very much the case with respect to our providing the time and energy for listening to *ourselves*.

Finding: Listening to Ourselves

Finding and nurturing a true sense of identity is an outgrowth of listening to ourselves and those people in our life who truly believe in us. To help people do this, I have encouraged them to find a "word" for themselves. This word should be 80 percent who they are already and 20 percent who they wish to become. I break it down this way so that people don't go to extremes. If, in reality, we are only 20 percent this type of person, then we may be reaching to become a person who we are not meant to be. On the other hand, if we are almost 100 percent this type of person, there is no room for growth, insight and development; we are too comfortable and stagnant.

This word or name should not be linked to a public image, a given image (like our own name and assigned role in the family or society) or even an artificial ideal image, for that matter. It should be a beautiful image of who the person can be as a part of the whole garden of creation. For those of us who are religious people, it is our name before God.

I encourage those whom I see for mentoring or in therapy to find a word as a way to center themselves. It is also important for those of us who are helpers and healers to have such an identity so that we can rest in it when we are in stressful psychological or challenging spiritual situations with others in need.

The search for a word can be an intriguing and exciting process. It is also a rather dynamic one, since our word evolves as we grow. While it won't change overnight or possibly for years, it is something that helps us gauge where we need to develop and blossom spiritually and psychologically.

I remember when I first came upon this idea for myself, I shared with my wife, "I have a new name!" She was used to such outrageous pronouncements on my part, so she simply said, "Oh, what is it?"

I replied that it was "enthusiasm"! She looked at me and said, "Well, I really don't care for it."

To which I replied: "Well, I didn't mean for this to be a dialogue. What I had in mind is that I would mention my newfound name and you would applaud."

After we finished teasing each other about my original selection, we each reflected again on which word seemed apropos and why. She explained to me that "enthusiasm" did not seem to be a deep and large enough word to reflect what she and others saw in me. Finally, after some discussion, "vitality" seemed to be a better choice. Given who we both felt I was, it was a word that would call me to be all that I could be without embarrassing me regarding where I was at this point in life. It was a word that named much of who I enjoyed being, while still encouraging me to be more sensitive to those areas that blocked my sense of vitality.

Being

As we listen to our heart and find a sense of identity (our *word*) in which to rest and bring to reflection or prayer, we then can act out of that identity in a true and spontaneous way. Rather than drifting or fighting with life, we can flow with it naturally; this is truly being who we can be in life.

I remember going to an elementary school to give a workshop on burnout to the teachers. As soon as I turned the corner, I could see what looked to be a little kindergarten boy coming down the hall. When he got close, I realized that he had his shoes on the wrong feet. I said to him, "Look at your shoes." He looked down, nodded, looked up at me, smiled and kept walking— or rather wob-bling— down the hall.

Without a sense of who we are, we wobble with the wrong iden-tity as well. We take for granted that we know who we are. We make the mistake of never taking the time to listen to, find and nurture who we are *now,* at this stage of our lives.

Yet, with some courage and reflection, we can discover not only who we are, but revel in the beauty that we find in ourselves so that we can share it freely with others. To do this, however, takes a bit of effort. It likewise requires a quiet little place in our lives where our spirit can breathe deeply, rest and learn. In the next chapter we will journey to such a place.

. . . .

FOR REFLECTION...

The real impact we have on others and that others have on us is often too subtle to be articulated. This impact that leaves us "speechless" is experienced as a gentle, affirming presence. Who are the mentors, teachers and guides who have nudged or pushed you toward healthy self-respect? What did they do to move you in this positive direction?

How can you hone your listening skills so as to improve the accuracy of your own interior "music" as well as the "music" that others play for themselves?

3. A Quiet Little Place...
to Breathe Deeply

→

I once remember walking past a vast, well-developed English garden. Stopping, I could see the roses, unruly flowering bushes and established, deep green ground cover. Moss and heather, trellises and a pond with a bubbling waterfall filled with koi and flowering water lilies made me feel good just to be there. I felt at home, peaceful.

Then, off in the distance I could see a little sign stuck into the ground. It was near one of the entrances to a back path. I was intrigued by what it might say. When I walked over, I had to get on my knees to read it. The message was simple:

> There is always music in the garden
> amongst the trees...
> But your heart must be quiet
> to hear it.

Silent places allow us to breathe deeply, to take in little messages of self-respect from our inner selves. They give us the gentle space to feel the basic spiritual themes that will put us back on the path when we are lost. They help us, like the young boy Samuel in the Bible, to listen to our God speak softly to us in a small voice that too much anxiety and inner noise can often drown out.

Quiet places are not simply there for escape from our crazy

lives. (Although, occasionally, it is a wise thing to RUN AWAY!) Instead, little places of silence allow us to take a step back, to begin a "minisabbatical," so that we can sit, rest, think, reassess and (as was just noted in the last chapter) *listen*. This need is truly felt when we are emotionally and spiritually exhausted and realize that we have fallen off the path of single-heartedness and simplicity. It helps us see the truth about our condition when we fall prey to compulsive activity and are running to our grave with no sense of serenity or clarity. One of the times that I recognized I was doing this was about fifteen years ago. I was feeling terribly burned out, being torn as I was in many different directions by the many varied demands of others and my own rigid conscience and fears. In trying to do good things as well as to be present to so many needy people, I myself had become needy and confused.

I knew that I had to do something about it. As someone interested in the integration of psychology and spirituality, to what "mountain" would I go for encouragement and guidance? Who would be the person who could respond to both my emotional needs and the shakiness in my own inner life? I had to take time out and visit someone who was a sage, a teacher, or, in Japanese, a spiritual *sansei*. Again, the question hung in the air: Who could do this for me? Furthermore, how could I arrange such a visit?

After checking my college travel budget, I noticed that there was some money in it to attend conferences. I finally chose someone to visit whose work I had read and loved. I contacted him and found out, much to my surprise, that my visit would be welcomed. I then arranged for the trip, and within one month, I found myself in Boston, where I spent a quiet afternoon and evening in anticipation of my meeting.

The next morning I got up and had breakfast. After that, I walked along the Charles River to Harvard. Then I made a right at Harvard Square, walked several more blocks and found an unassuming apartment building. I entered the little lobby and looked into the mailbox where I was told I would find the key to the front door. This arrangement was necessary, as I had been warned in a letter that the bell did not work.

I climbed three sets of stairs, knocked on the door and was greeted by a person who had for years mentored me through his writings. For about one and one-half hours, I had the wonderful opportunity to meet with the spiritual guide Henri Nouwen.

We spoke mostly about my work, particularly about my writing. In speaking about these efforts, he also helped me to reflect then and later about my life. I was preparing a manuscript tentatively titled *Relationships: Nurturing the Gift of Availability.* He questioned me quite directly about how I was avoiding the realities and problems of availability.

In addition, we spoke about the wonderful biblical image of "pruning" and how that helps increase the fruit and expand the blossoms when it is done right. His impact was so profound that I changed the title of the book to *Availability: The Problem and the Gift* before Paulist Press published it. What he taught me about the importance of balance came through loud and clear and has stayed with me long after that visit.

However, the key part of the meeting for me occurred when I was about to leave. I realized that I had not asked him directly about what he could suggest to help me to further deepen and nourish my inner life. I wanted his guidance so that I could get hold of a place in myself that would be sturdy. Using the imagery from his writings, I wanted to find a stream within myself from which I could drink when I needed to quench my thirst for peace and joy, especially during dry and upsetting times. I desperately needed a gentle inner place to be with my own sense of identity and beauty as well as to meet others— including the living God.

Then, I remembered that when Henri was with Mother Teresa of Calcutta, years prior to this, he had asked her what he should do to ensure that his life as a priest would be a rich and good one. I thought that I would do the same with him, and so I said, "Before I leave, what one thing can you suggest to me that will keep me alive spiritually and psychologically? What is the most important thing that I must do to be a person of peace so that I can reach out to others and not be swept under myself?"

He said, "Well, there is probably so much I could suggest; I'm not exactly sure what to say at this point." In saying this, he looked as if he would then show me to the door. However, I was determined to get "a word" from this contemporary spiritual Abba. Thus, I gave him a look that essentially said, "I'm not leaving until you bless me with a word of guidance."

I think that he saw this look, because he stopped, thought a few moments, probably decided he didn't want to assume the role of the angel being tackled by the spiritual journeyer Jacob, and then spoke to me directly from his heart:

> Take a few moments every morning in silence and solitude. Read a few passages from Scripture. If you have a daily book of biblical readings or a lectionary, use that. Then once you have read these words from Scripture, sit quietly and let them nurture you in silence. Do this every day without fail and you shall be all right.

Then I left with his words in my heart and a beautifully inscribed copy of a book entitled *Desert Wisdom,* for which he wrote the foreword. In it he wrote, "In gratitude for your visit...Henri Nouwen." Today, I still have this book as well as other ones he sent me with notes in them. I am eternally grateful for his suggestion regarding how to start each day. Indeed, going off to a quiet place to pray does keep a continually flowing fresh stream of spiritual peace in my life. What could be more important than that?

The Benefits of Silence and Solitude

The value of solitude has only recently been noted in the field of psychology. A recent book on the topic, authored by Anthony Storr notes:

> Modern psychotherapists, including myself have taken as their criterion of emotional maturity the capacity of the individual to make mature relationships on equal terms. With few exceptions, psychotherapists have omitted to consider the fact that the capacity to be alone is also an aspect of emotional maturity.[5]

In this work, he also cites the experiences of Admiral Byrd in his search for solitude as an example of an individual who recognized its value and much later in his life was even able to capitalize upon it. Byrd sought to be by himself in order to "know the kind of experience to the full, to be by himself for a while and to taste peace and quiet and solitude long enough to find out how good they really are."[6] Years later he was also to reflect: "I did take away something that I had not fully possessed before: appreciation of the sheer beauty and miracle of being alive, and a humble set of values...civilization has not altered my ideas. I live more simply now, and with more peace."[7]

We must be able to hear our own inner voice instead of only our anxieties and the myriad fearful and negative voices that fill our outer world at home, in the classroom, at places of amusement and that even dominate our places of worship! But in today's active life, where and when do we find such space? Furthermore, given our lack of experience with it, how will we spend this time alone in a way that is renewing? We don't want to let it be just a time for moody introspection or vengeful musings about how we have been mistreated in life.

Maybe what Henri Nouwen suggested to me would be good for many of us as a way to structure some quiet time alone. We can consider the following:

— Sit with sacred Scriptures or another valued book of wisdom and read a little bit of it.

— Let the words settle upon us like a nest, so that we can then take at least two minutes to be alone with true wisdom, allowing it to seep into us.

— Later (as we become comfortable with it), approach such a gentle space for more time— say twenty minutes in the morning and a slightly shorter period at night.

The benefits are certainly there if we approach such a place, not with a sense of duty, but as a time for returning to our self; it will become a gentle place of reassurance, reassessment and peace. Time spent in silence and solitude on a regular basis can effect us in the following ways:

Sharpen our sense of clarity about the life we are living and the choices we are making;

Enhance our attitude of simplicity;

Increase our humility and help us avoid unnecessary arrogance by allowing time to examine the defenses and games we play (these often surface for us to see during quiet times);

Let us enjoy our relationship with ourselves more;

Decrease our dependence on the reinforcement of others;

Enable us to recognize our own areas of anger, entitlement, greed and cowardice (given the opportunity to quietly review the day's activities and our reaction to them);

Protect our own inner fire so that we can reach out without being pulled down;

Help us to accept change and loss;

Make us more sensitive to the compulsions in our lives;

Experience the importance of love and acceptance (which are fruits of the contemplative life) and acknowledge the silliness and waste involved in condemning self and judging others;

Allow us to hear the gentle inner voice that reflects the spiritual sound of authenticity and the heart of our living faith; and

Help us to respect the need to take time to strengthen our own inner space so that we can, in turn, be more sensitive to the contemplative presence of others.

In other words, taking quiet time in solitude and silence during each day can provide us with a place to breathe deeply so that we can have the strength to know better how—in scriptural terms—"to live simply, love tenderly, and walk humbly with our God" (Mi 6:8).

Yet, even when we know the true value of silence and solitude, we run from it. For us, to value the quiet in our lives, we must know not only what these periods can do for us but also (as we will see in the next chapter) be able to really appreciate *what price they may extract from us.* Otherwise, we will just continue to speak about silence and solitude wistfully as something wonderful and never enjoy what this well of truth and support can offer us. We will be like people who speak more about prayer than they actually pray. On the other hand, true people of silence know the challenges that come with being quietly present in today's noisy, distracting world. They are aware of the psychological challenges of spiritual intimacy, and so we must become aware of them as well.

. . . .

FOR REFLECTION...

Finding a "place" of silence and solitude requires more than separating ourselves from the company of others. We can go off to a quiet room and yet be bombarded by a cacophony of inner voices all vying for attention. How have you sought/found quiet places of true solitude in your life? Why are such "escapes" necessary for a balanced life?

What is the lure of silence? What frightens you about it? Why are you simultaneously drawn to and resistant to silence and solitude?

4. In Solitude: A "Good Loneliness"

→

Silence speaks eloquently in solitude; listening quietly to our hearts allows us to walk unprotected and unguarded with the Truth in our inner "garden." However, this time of quiet listening may also present us with a challenge: It may bring us to a place of loneliness and vulnerability, open us to a new recognition of hidden lies. So, although the process of taking time away from our daily activities is essential and good, there are elements with which we will find it difficult to deal once we embrace silence and solitude. We should know about this challenging reality so that the unconscious hesitancy to take quiet time doesn't surprise us and totally undermine our efforts to seek solitude. Time away for reflection is too valuable to lose because of ignorance or hidden anxiety.

Our natural tendency is to actively avoid silence and time alone. Distracting and amusing ourselves with activities is a much more common practice than being involved on a regular basis in the process of reflection and prayer. Prayer confronts us with the awkward way we often live out our days; likewise, in silence, we are reminded of our mortality. Consequently, talking about prayer is a lot easier than praying. Thus, when we seek to establish a life of reflection and prayer or further develop the prayer life we have, we must realize that the process won't go as smoothly as we'd like. A road sign at the beginning of a highway construction site outside of Washington, D.C. warns:

BE PREPARED TO BE FRUSTRATED!

As we travel along the roadway of prayer, the same advice is often appropriate. The difficult experiences we encounter during periods of solitude need not be considered negative even if initially we feel that they are. If we neither avoid nor run away from them, we can learn to understand and appreciate the constructive moments of our periods of loneliness, vulnerability and discovery.

For instance, a number of years ago, as I was walking down a winding Virginia road with a mentor, I shared with him an unusual experience I had during my quiet time. I said to him, "My life is basically quite good. I don't feel deprived or needy. Instead, most of the time I feel grateful and challenged. However, lately in my quiet time of reflection, I have felt a sense of wistful loneliness, like something was missing. I felt a light ache of emptiness passing through my stomach...that something real, important and basic was missing, and I deeply yearned for it—whatever this 'it' was."

His response surprised me. He did not brush off my experience as of no consequence, advise that it would pass shortly or tell me how to combat it. Instead he said, "That's good. The loneliness that you describe is meant to remind you that your heart will not be ultimately satisfied by anyone or anything now in this life. Your loneliness also reminds you that even though you may distract yourself with many things and people— even lovely ones—your sense of being at home can only be given by something deeper, greater...what you and I call 'God.'

"And so, the loneliness will allow you to enjoy people, things and life in general *in their proper perspective.* As a result, you can enjoy the people and gifts in life, but they will not become idols for you because your loneliness will teach you they can never be equal to a loving, living God. This will also open you up to seek a deeper relationship with God within your inner core.

"Then, rather than being tempted to 'set up tents' prematurely when you have wonderful experiences or relationships, you will have the freedom to enjoy them without being captured and controlled by your desire for them. Therefore, the loneliness will keep your heart open, aware; your journey will continue with a sense of passion and expectancy. That is, if you let it and don't try to avoid or 'medicate' such initially troubling feelings with activities, distractions or work."

Andrew Harvey, in his famous book *A Journey to Ladakh,* approaches this feeling from a Buddhist perspective by offering a response he received from someone with whom he shared a similar situation:

> As we parted, he hugged me and said, "You smile a great deal and you listen well, but I see that somewhere you are sad. I see nothing has satisfied you...."
> I started to protest.
> "No," he said, "nothing has satisfied you, not your work, not your friendships, not all your learning and traveling. And that is good. You are ready to learn something new. Your sadness has made you empty; your sadness has made you open!"[8]

The Strength of Interior Vulnerability

Solitude, reflection and prayer are not only places that welcome loneliness. Quiet periods may also prove to be times of great vulnerability. Such vulnerability may lead to greater inner strength if given a chance to be experienced rather than avoided. This opportunity is possible because in being vulnerable and humble (not a popular word today), we can be open to the spiritual movements in our lives. Thus we will not only recognize our own strengths, but also see when and where we need help from others—including God.

Recently, I visited Birmingham, Alabama, and had a chance to see the parish where Martin Luther King, Jr., was pastor. It was in the back of that church where the plan for the bus boycott was formulated after Rosa Parks refused to move to the back of the bus. As

I stood there in front of the church, I remembered something that Martin Luther King, Jr., had shared about the early days of his struggle for equality.

There was a period at the beginning of the nonviolent movement when, in prayer, King admitted that he felt fearful, depleted, exhausted, undone. In a quiet moment alone, he told God that he didn't have the energy to continue. Then, after he had emptied his heart in prayer, he said that he finally surrendered and agreed that "Thy will be done." Upon doing this, he said that he felt the presence of God in his life as never before.

Several days after this experience, while he was on the road, his house was bombed. He later told others that because of his recent prayer experience, this incident neither made him more fearful, nor did it have the major negative impact it probably would have had otherwise. On the contrary, after his transforming encounter in solitude with God, he felt prepared to continue with his mission. And, as we know, he was able to go on; not only did he have the energy to lead but to lead in a way that the world will never forget.

A Psychological Vacuum

As well as opening us to loneliness and vulnerability, silence and solitude can form a psychological vacuum into which many feelings, memories and awarenesses (which lie just below the surface in the preconscious) may be encouraged to surface. At such times as these, we are being called in reflection and prayer to face the truths about ourselves that for some unconscious reason we may have put aside, denied or diminished.

Having such truths surface is not terrible, of course, especially if we remember that many of these insights will actually be helpful rather than harmful. The only "damage" is that which will be suffered by the false image of ourselves that we have created because we haven't been willing to trust in our own inherent value. So by spending time in silence and solitude, we will be able to see the extent to which our self-worth has, to this point, been built upon a foundation of sand. We will come to recognize that our sense of self-worth is dependent in an exaggerated way on praise by others, positive experiences we have (including ones in prayer and meditation) and a list of other past achievements. Though unpleasant, finding out this truth is still quite life-giving. Such an epiphany allows us to rediscover a sense of self and worth grounded in true self-respect. We then can come to understand that real self-respect is based on a deep, concrete trust in the inherent spiritual value of being a human person rather than on specific accomplishments or the reception of kudos from others.

Arriving at this point of insight is not a magical process. The desire to be a person who is solidly aware of self-worth no matter what others say or do, no matter what mistakes or shameful things we might do, cannot thrive just as a wishful thought. It has to be welcomed and passionately sought in silence and solitude, that place in which a strong and healthy attitude toward *all* of life is formed.

The Quiet Stream Deep Within— Building a Simple and Strong Spiritual Life

In order to nurture an inner life that is real and vibrant— one without which we may exist but never truly *live*—we need to avoid two extremes. The first is the belief that we can live a spiritual life easily and without taking the time to create a structure that enables us to better listen to the quiet little voice of Truth.

If we merely feel that "our work is our prayer," reflect only when the feeling prompts us to do so or leave quiet reflection solely for unique, designated times during the day or week (Sunday?), we will then be left with an appropriately limited legacy; namely, an artificial, narrow, undemanding relationship with our inner selves and with God.

On the other hand, some signs that a well-grounded life of reflection is in place are these:

— A willingness to see reflection or prayer in a broader perspective. Reflection is not simply asking God for help or uttering general platitudes of gratitude and vague notations of repentance that sound like a governmental admission of wrongdoing. Rather, words of praise, gratitude, sorrow and request represent a balanced, honest, concrete approach to a real relationship between God and the genuine core of our real selves.

— Time, our most valuable possession, spent regularly being quietly alone with God, reading sacred scripture and spiritual writings, and sharing our faith with others;

— A structure to our daily routine based on *regular* times of prayer — in the morning and evening, as well as other brief periods of recollection during the day; and

— Constant attempts to discern whether our behavior is in line with what we believe and whether our faith is influencing the decisions we are making now and for the future.

It is important to realize that while exercising discipline and conscious attention to a life of prayer helps avoid the dangers of allowing laxity and spiritual wistfulness from quietly ruling our life without our knowledge, providing such a structure paradoxically sets the stage for a second extreme, namely, an overreliance on ourselves and our discipline of prayer.

In many instances, we who meditate, study scripture and have a regular routine of faith-filled attention to life often lament that something is still missing at the heart of our spiritual life. We feel that our regimen of reflection is not working as well as we think it should. If we are religious people, we might even complain quietly that God is hiding from us.

There are naturally many reasons why we may feel this way. Consequently, there are probably an equal number of ways (if not more) that we could attack this problem. However, in a predominance of cases, there is one recognition that would help move the logjam of experience that we are having. We need to recall and meditate upon the central role that possessing an attitude of love should have in our spiritual life.

Making adjustments in our own life is important. It's also true that having courage in how we approach life's decisions and our relationship with self and God in the quiet moments of our day is essential. Moreover, it is important to remember that in seeking to *deepen our love* in prayer, we come to recognize any lack of that love in ourselves. As we progress in the process, the music and the lyrics of a relationship between the true self and the living God will finally be heard. It is in loving that we realize that we are in an open relationship in which God has a role as well.

The reason we may resist this awareness is that it may require us to see our own *lack* of love...our barrenness...our manipulating nature...our lack of faith...our desire to control life...our failure to believe, really believe that we are going to die someday, and life is going to go on without us. Love in the concrete is not as pleasing as the ending of an old movie. Real love, though, leaves us a good deal more satisfied and nourished than just pondering it in the abstract. Abstract love is like a menu in a window of a fine restaurant; it may whet the appetite, but it does nothing to quiet our actual hunger.

When we seek to love ourselves truly and to love the Source of Creation, we will feel energized even in our dryness; we will feel called even when we don't know the exact direction; we will feel hopeful even during anxious, wakeful moments of the night. Why? Because we will know we are on a real journey of faith and because of it, no matter what happens, we will see new things that will help us. We will learn. We will have more questions. *We will be alive!*

. . . .

FOR REFLECTION...

How have your experiences of loneliness and vulnerability changed your self-understanding?

What opportunities do you see for spiritual growth in these so-called "negative" experiences of loneliness and vulnerability?

5. Relationships and Friendships

→

Once while passing an office cubicle, I saw a little frayed sign with the following words on it:

> A friend knows the song in your heart
> and can sing it back to you
> when you have forgotten how it goes.

I have never forgotten this quote. I have included it in past books as well as in many of my lectures. When I share it with students they remark long after the end of the course that these words have stayed with them. The reason may be that this saying reminds us of the cornerstone that friendship plays in a life that is both gentle and passionate. How can we enjoy life without the presence of good friends?

Unfortunately, friendship is something we often take for granted. If asked about our relationships we say, "Oh yes, I value my friends." But do we intentionally look at this arena when considering our own spiritual growth and sense of compassion? Do we know which friends grace us? On the other hand, are we aware of those whom we encounter, who, for some unconscious reason, seem to despise the center of our souls?

Experiences of friendship can crop up anywhere. They can be beacons to provide us with a sense of what is important in life. By the same token, if they are not reflected upon in order to provide lasting insight, they merely may be experiences that make us feel good for the moment, rather than enlightening us as epiphanies of new wisdom. In essence, even fleeting encounters can teach us something *if we are awake to the lesson that is taking place in the relationship.*

Many years back, as mentioned earlier, I worked in the Amish country of Pennsylvania. You'll probably remember that part of this work included making rounds on Sunday morning in a hospital in Lancaster County. Going out to the hospital early in the morning along the old Lincoln Highway was a quick trip. I enjoyed the quiet, easy ride at that hour. About fifteen minutes from the hospital, though, I would encounter Amish buggies that slowed the end of the trip to a crawl.

Once at the hospital, the visits were usually straightforward. In addition to the patients in the psychiatry unit, there were some medical patients in intensive care or on other floors for whom we were providing consultant services. Although I liked the work, I still remember one time when I didn't want to go. It had been a long week that included some work on Saturday. Understandably, my hopes were that the rounds could be done quickly so that I would have most of Sunday free.

At the start of my rounds, I visited a young Amish boy who had been in an accident. He looked a bit frightened, and when I was in the room, I did most of the talking. Keeping a relaxed look, I sat down and chatted as if I had all day in the hope that I could put him at ease with me and his situation. After being there a while, I stood up and said, "I'll stop back again to see you before I leave," and I smiled. He looked up and said, "OK." My thought as I left him was, "Poor kid. He's still scared from the trauma of the accident."

When I moved on to see the other patients, I put him out of my mind. Our encounter had slipped my mind so much so that when I finished the last visit, I went out to my car, forgetting my promise to return and see the young boy before leaving. Suddenly, just as I was getting in the car, I remembered him and I returned to the hospital.

I said, "Bet you thought I had forgotten you." In response, he looked up, briefly smiled, and said, "No, I knew you'd come back." His comment and the small pained smile on his face made me see how we often don't see our impact on other people and the potential joy present in even brief, passing relationships.

What struck me at that moment was both simple and profound: This little epiphany was something important to remember. I could let it go as a nice but fleeting experience of meeting someone in need, or I could see it as a beacon shining on such temporary meetings with others, demonstrating how important these happenstance moments are if we recognize them, if we see their deep value.

Chance meetings during our day can be times of awakening to what is important; on the other hand, we can be semioblivious to them. Either we are too busily preoccupied with our own little worlds to recognize them as opportunities for "awareness," or we don't see them as having "real" value when compared with long, deep conversations with someone we've known a long time.

Preconceived notions of relationship prevent us from enjoying and receiving real wisdom in our day-to-day meetings. As a matter of fact, when we truly are open to a wider sense of what relationships can be for us if we nurture those around us (even when we feel we are in the position of "giving to" or teaching someone), we may be surprised by what we can learn. The following story of a Catholic nun from the United States illustrates this clearly:

> I had been two years in Malawi and was feeling very home-sick. I had a free period and went to the library where I found a *Time-Life* volume on New York City—my hometown. As I gazed out the window at the surrounding village with its neat huts and rows and rows of young maize plants just beginning to shoot forth from the parched, red clay earth, I held the book tightly and tears came to my eyes. How did I

get here? What was I doing here? I opened the book and flipped through its pages. As I focused on Broadway and 42nd Street, with its towering buildings, glitzy lights and traffic jams, into the room walked barefoot Ekalena, a far cry from the metropolitan folk passing each other unknowingly on the busy city street. Ekalena came over to greet me in gracious African fashion, for an African always acknowledges the presence of the other. "Would you care to see a picture of my village?" I asked. Enthusiastically, she took the book and stared at the picture for quite some time. I was getting excited and eager to *teach her* what the rest of the world was like. She handed the book back to me with questioning sadness in her eyes and said, "But where is your garden?"[9]

In this relationship, Sister felt she would be the one to teach. Instead, this young woman whom she sought to educate and enlighten gave her a simple question to ponder concerning what is truly important in life. But, at least Sister could learn. The question for us is twofold: Do we have the openness to learn as well? Will we let others point out what "gardens" are missing in our lives amidst our success, accomplishments and fears, the gardens that need to be planted so that we can be nourished by them?

Developing a Community of Friends

As well as having and encouraging openness, our community of friends must be richly gifted. It must:

— include opportunities both to give and receive;

— be heterogeneous enough for us not to stagnate;

— have a balance of voices (prophetic, supportive, humorous, spiritual) so that we can have the different facets of ourselves fed and challenged. (This is discussed further in my little book with Robert M. Hamma entitled *A Circle of Friends*.)

In addition to finding friends for the journey, we must be content to be vulnerable and humble rather than grasping and needy. In most cases it is true that the healthier and gentler we are, the more we will attract healthier friends. Such a stance will also allow what is good in others to be revealed, when the time and circumstances are right.

When I was in Thailand leading a retreat, I met a missionary who worked in Bangladesh. He had a fascinating background, and because of his deeply caring attitude, had met many interesting people throughout his life. One of these people was Mother Teresa of Calcutta. One story he tells about her involves the time she went begging during a famine in the area where she taught in the war-torn Bengal of 1943.

The students were hungry and there was no money to buy food to feed them. When reaching out to a rich gentleman from the area for help, he spat on her. To this she simply responded: "That was for me. Now what are you going to give me for my girls?" He was so moved by her humility that he not only gave her alms, he also became a lifelong supporter and friend.[10]

Friendship is a place that many of us do not know fully because we have a preconceived notion of what it looks like in advance. Yet, when we have a good relationship with our *selves* and if we are spiritually connected with our God, the notion of friendship widens. Possibilities open and we are fed because of them. However, openness does not mean being totally indiscriminate in how we reach out to others. Such forms of no-boundary relationships help no one.

A Healthy Distance

Our life and spirituality are deepened by compassion and friendship but can be wrecked by the hazards of compulsive giving.

Learning to be a powerful presence to others is essential if we are to be happy, but giving away the source of our passion and energy is no gift to anyone—especially ourselves.

Maintaining a healthy distance includes the following:

— an appreciation of the power of the negative;

— a willingness to be detached enough to care;

— a nuanced sense of what angry people are experiencing;

— an acceptance of people's right to be where they are (even though they are not where we would like them to be!)

The Power of the Negative

During the bloody civil war between the Hutus and the Tutsis in Rwanda, I debriefed several of the evacuated relief workers. In the midst of one of the interviews, I noticed that I was holding onto the arms of my chair very firmly. In young people's parlance a while back, I was "white-knuckling" it.

After this poignant session was over, I did a counter-transferential review. In other words, I reflected on my feelings and reactions to see what I could understand about the person seeing me, the interaction in general, and what I might learn about myself.

The first and most obvious thing that struck me was my grasping of the arm of my chair. Why had I done that? What had caused me to become upset, angry or afraid? After imaging myself back in the room and reflecting on what was going on within myself as well as on the content and feeling of what the person was saying to me, it hit me. The graphic stories made me so uncomfortable that I was frightened, and I felt that if I were not careful, I might be pulled into the vortex of darkness.

I was picking up the person's sense of helplessness, fear, insecurity and trauma. Not only had the people of Rwanda been traumatized, but also the individuals who worked with them were themselves placed on the psychological edge. In turn, I was also exposed to a dramatic sense of the terrible acts we as people can do to each other under certain highly stressful circumstances.

Understanding what went on was as important a step for me as it was for my patients. In addition, finding a support system for myself so that I could debrief with another person was essential. Moreover, on a more basic level, I realized again a basic principle of friendship: Whether we encounter trauma or not, it is important for us to have people to talk to during and after a full day of involvement in the world. We need to have people who will listen to our story and help us delve more deeply into the emotions of the day so that we can finally put them aside rather than have them continue to churn inside. If the unresolved emotions remain, they will eventually come out in an array of psychological and physical symptoms and disorders.

Respect for the negative should also include an appreciation of the strength of despair, despondency and cynicism in the world. From the morning news shows that seek to find a sensational negative side to almost any story, to the very needy and angry people in the world who destablize many of us by their actions and reactions, we are exposed to negative "psychological viruses." When frustrated counseling students are psychologically thrown about by bright, demanding clients, I often say to them, "Please remember, on any given day a person's pathology can be more powerful than your health. However, in the long run, your health will make a difference in this person's life in some way."

Cynical people in our family, on the job or in our general environment are sometimes suffering from a long-term personality disorder that has been honed to a razor's edge after a lifetime of anxiety, neediness and stress. They may appear like birds with broken wings because of their vulnerability, but their fears and neediness can also bare their teeth in such a way that almost no matter what we do, they will respond in ways that tell us in no uncertain terms: you are not doing enough for me.

This is not so surprising since they themselves have had childhoods shot through with trauma and instability. Our response must be a faithfulness that is based on a clear recognition that we can do only what is within our power. By respecting negativity in all its forms, we can minimize the pain that can be exacted upon us as we relate with such persons. Also, this sense of respect will help us to keep perspective so that we are willing to stay the course with people who need us but are trying simultaneously in so many ways to push us away.

Detachment

Part of the way we can keep perspective is to value a certain amount of detachment. This is necessary so that we don't get pulled down into the quicksand of emotions that the person with whom we are interacting may be experiencing at the moment.

There is an old Russian proverb that blandly states, "When you live next to the cemetery, you can't cry for everyone who dies." We need to recognize that caring for others is not tantamount to being as miserable or as needy as they are. After all, what would such suffering achieve?

Once an acquaintance whom we hadn't seen in ten years came over to our home. After the usual pleasantries, he launched into a very sad story about how his wife of two years had left him for another man. The story was very poignant and the poor man was suffering a great deal. During the interaction, a mutual friend of ours, who was also visiting, had tears in her eyes. Both she and our friend cried over the shock of this sad parting and the dissolution of the marriage he had so badly wanted.

After he left, we had dinner. During the meal she asked, "I felt so sorry for Tim. But as I looked at you, there wasn't a tear in your eyes. Why?"

"Well, I did feel really sad for him. What a terrible shock for him; he loved her so much. However, I also wanted to be of some help to him. He needed to see some things in a different perspective. He needed greater clarity and hope. I felt that if I got too involved with him and overly empathic, I would be so down over it that I wouldn't be detached enough to help. It's the old story of the surgeon. You don't want your surgeon to be so upset over your physical condition that the scalpel shakes in his hand. I think that the same can be said about the person doing psychological and spiritual counseling. It's not that you don't get upset at times, but you try to minimize it during the time you are reaching out. You can do the personal debriefing later, as we are doing now."

A Nuanced Sense of Anger

Distancing is a valuable factor in reaching out because it allows us to see people in a different light. This is especially the case with respect to anger. Often, I have either personalized other people's anger or been blown over by it. The result is that I have pulled back or retaliated. Anger is nothing but a pointer. It shows us that people are afraid, hurt, under great stress, insecure or destabilized in some way. But if we are angry too we will fail to see the source of the other person's hostile feelings and behavior.

I'll often tell teachers that they must learn to deal with anger in parents, children and fellow educators. I want them to recognize that anger is often covering something else, and that they shouldn't seek to attack in return. However, and it is a big "however," we also need to be careful not to give away to angry people our power to be enthusiastic, encouraging, hopeful and passionate.

In the case of teachers, I warn them that other teachers who are angry may have experienced difficulties on the job or in their home life, past or present; I warn them not to add to their colleagues' grief. By the same token, burnout is contagious, so in the process of interacting with angry persons we must take care not to give away our happiness just because they are upset or have temporarily given up.

Acceptance

In line with this is a caution I alluded to earlier: We must learn to accept people not only for who they are, but also for their right to be where they are— even if, especially if, they are not where we want them to be! This does not mean that we shouldn't continue to reach out to help them get more out of life. Those who shut themselves off and distance people through their negativity are the very ones who need from us a warm presence and an effort to connect.

But we must also have low expectations and high hopes. In other words, we must never stop believing in possibilities for such people, but neither should we get discouraged if the adults with whom we deal act like young adolescents or seem resistant to new ideas.

We are all stubborn in our own ways. We all avoid really seeing the possibilities of new experiences. We can see this symbolically with respect to tastes in clothing and food. Often, when people suggest that I buy something that is not the very same colors I have in my wardrobe, I say, "Oh, I don't like that color and I don't think I look good in it." What I am really saying is this: "I stopped considering new possibilities years ago in colors, designs, and unfortunately, in life."

Other people do the same with regard to food as I do with my selection of clothes. I don't have this particular difficulty since I like most foods and will try almost anything a number of times. (Of course, this doesn't include Philadelphia scrapple!) But there are many people I know who have dug in their heels at the age of fifteen and won't try anything that didn't make the grade back then. I truly believe that it is not taste that is holding them back. Instead, as in the case of my resistance to trying other styles and colors, it is symbolic of a stubborn resistance to opening ourselves to new things in life.

Some Final Comments

Thus, giving freely and constantly to others without concern for receiving their gratitude, achieving results or compliance with our suggestions is an essential part of compassion. We need to do what we can for others. We also obviously need warm, caring and challenging friends in our own life—people who are excited about who we are and where we are "growing," spiritually and psychologically.

As was noted finally in this chapter and as we know from experience, we need to recognize that it is natural for some people to have unrealistic expectations of us. People often seem to be saying to us what the following Yiddish proverb demands: "Sleep faster...We need the pillows!"

In response, we need to be more like the Dalai Lama. He often had many, many demands on him and was asked how he handled them all and slept well at night. He indicated quite simply in the ordinary style that has made him so appreciated in the world that he did what he could during the day with complete sincerity. And once that was done, he let go. Such sincerity and a willingness to let go after we have done what we could—even if it didn't work out as others or we would have liked—are two important keys to compassion and the basis of good relationships.

. . . .

FOR REFLECTION...

What is your understanding of detachment and why is detachment so important to the helping relationship?

How can healthy detachment enhance your day-to-day relationships and friendships?

What role does friendship have in your life and why is it important for at least some of your friendships to move deeper than the superficial/social dimension?

6. Silent Hope

→

The contemplative Thomas Merton once remarked in the stark, honest way for which he was best known:

> True love and prayer are learned
> when love becomes impossible
> and the heart has turned to stone.[11]

Looking at it another way, I think that he was recognizing in a very unvarnished way that pain and joy are often intimately related. They come together and are in the same world. Both belong to us. Being contemplatively sensitive to the realities of the world and our own day-to-day lives requires us to acknowledge and respect the pain while welcoming with open arms the joy...wherever it is.

Several years ago, I had the opportunity to make two trips to teach in New Zealand. On one of those visits, I was riding through the beautiful countryside of the North Island with a priest ordained less than one year. As we chatted during the ride, I was thoroughly struck by the vividly green hills. The wild, pastoral scene was also marked by bright yellow gauss that the farmers see as unwanted weeds, but that I viewed as a welcoming splash of shocking accents to the remarkable view from my car window.

The beauty that day would convince me that New Zealand must be one of the most beautiful countries in the world. Just when I would feel that I had a grip on the colors and textures of the landscape, they would change. Hundreds of grazing sheep would be replaced by herds of deer that were also being raised by farmers in a climate that seemed to favor all types of animals and plants.

Commenting on the beauty was almost impossible. When I finally did try to say something, the only thing that came out was, "It looks just like a postcard." (Sometimes it is best to keep one's mouth closed!)

However, this beauty was evident in more than the land. I met New Zealanders, including Maoris as well as the descendants of early settlers from England and Scotland and the families of past generations of mine workers from Ireland. Whether brief or extensive, every encounter with these New Zealanders was a great treat; they taught me about the richness of their history and simplicity of their outlook.

As this young priest and I drifted from topic to topic, one of the experiences he shared with me was a very poignant encounter he'd had with a recently married couple. The wife had just given birth to twins. Only one was born alive; the other was dead upon delivery.

As he went into the details of his visit to the hospital, what he shared seemed to me to be a paradigm for life: Pain and joy come together, and we need to face both directly.

A portion of what he told me is as follows:

I entered the hospital and found the couple together. We spoke for a moment or two and then went together to visit both the children. First we went downstairs to the morgue. The place was dreary, cold and depressing. We looked at the little baby on the slab and the three of us prayed and cried.

Then we walked up the stairs to the neonatal intensive care unit. The place was filled with bright colors and hope. Smiles were on the nurses and new parents' faces. In place of the stone silence in the basement, here children were crying, people laughing; there was life and joy here. Once again, we stopped at the side of one of their children. Once again, there were tears and prayers—but this time they were expressions of joy and gratitude.

Both experiences were from a seamless garment of emotions. As I walked up those stairs, it was like a resurrection experience. Both children were their children. Both the pain and the joy were there together. They couldn't be separated and we didn't try. They needed, no *we* needed, to face them fully, honestly and openly. I think we did and are better for it now...they as parents and I as a priest.

Feeling both joy and pain fully is essential if we are to be truly alive. When we experience pain, doubt and fear, we must not run from it. We must feel it and *then* let it flow away from us when it is possible. This "then," this moment of release, this opening for new possibilities cannot be rushed. It may take years to come but, pray God, *it doesn't take one second longer than is needed*.

In the early stages of pain, it is hard to hear the seemingly silent voices of love and hope. At one point in the semester when I was teaching a course at Princeton Theological Seminary, I spoke about *sophia* (wisdom), the feminine face of God from the Hebrew Scriptures. I emphasized what a relief it is to sit with and be embraced by this image of our wonderful, loving God. I then asked the students to image themselves loved in this way so that they could model it for those who needed to be in touch with such deep love during difficult times.

At the end of class, a female Presbyterian seminarian came up to me with tears in her eyes and asked, "Do you really believe what you just said about God loving us?" I looked at her and quietly said: "Yes, I do." She simply nodded and said, "Thank you," and went on to her next class. It was obvious that her soul had been suffering for a long time.

It is very difficult to accept love and embrace hope when all is dark. Darkness is like hunger; you never forget either if you have ever been without food or felt despair. We must also remember that there is a wide, wide divide between someone who is in darkness and the loving companions walking with this person.

As one abuse victim described it to me: "When you are crawling on your belly, hope seems far off. The person without hope is silently screaming, 'Don't you understand my pain? Don't you see that all the suffering I face is unavoidable? Don't you see that I would love to trust something, someone…even you, but I am too frightened?' "

In a small way, this message was also brought across to me by a patient who had been confronting a mild depression. It was Christmastide, and she surprised me with a comment made almost sarcastically, "I'll bet you are the type that really enjoys Christmas!"

In response, I said with a smile, "Well, up to this point, I had planned to enjoy it. But now I don't know." She laughed a little, accustomed by now to my occasionally interjecting my light style into our sessions. Then I added more seriously, "What about you? What's holding you back from enjoying your time away from your work at the hospital?"

She said: "I am going home to be with my parents. How could I possibly enjoy anything with them—much less Christmas?"

To this I responded with a little smile on my face, "I'll tell you what. If you enjoy yourself this Christmas, I won't tell anybody."

Used to my teasing during the therapy sessions, she said in return: "All right, I'll bite. What is that supposed to mean?"

At this point, I got serious and said, "If anyone this Christmas deserves to eke out some measure of enjoyment, it is you. You have been through such a gray period in your life. Any joy you can get would be a wonderful respite for you, and I want you to have it. If you can enjoy trimming the tree, then do it. If you can find pleasure in walking through a store or visiting a friend, then do it. Make a list of even the smallest things you can take pleasure in and do them. Don't let anyone stop you by things said or looks given.

"Also, in your situation, it is common to fear that if you start feeling good, people who have stood by you during your depression might say, 'Oh, she's fine now. Look at how she is enjoying herself and feeling better this Christmas.' This may then produce the deep concern in you that once they see you doing well, they will then feel free to pull back and abandon you. But I want you to know that even when you are in a better place than you are now and are tempted in your own mind to set aside these difficult periods in your life, *I will never forget what you have been through. I will remember your pain.*

"But for now, let's make a pact that you will seek any chance to gain some sense of joy from any oasis possible in your desert. Let's spend the rest of today looking for ways you can experience some of the joy you deserve this Christmas."

If There's a Beginning, Then...

Silent hope is also more visible when we are able to see things in context. If we can trace our pain, see the details that paralleled its beginning, find out what our perceptions are regarding the experience we have had, and then reflect on how we now feel about it, we will glean a great deal of information that can be of use. In turn, this knowledge will also instill the seeds of hope.

Early in my work as a therapist, I learned the importance of searching out a concrete map of a person's pain. I remember one occasion in particular when I was presenting to my colleagues and the supervising psychiatrist a case involving a medical student who was experiencing a sense of depression. Being a new therapist, I made the sessions sound like a caricature of what Carl Rogers might have said given his nondirective style.

The patient would say, "I feel depressed." I would answer with the brilliant statement, "You seem down." She would go on and report that she was "in the pits." I would counter with, "Yes, you seem really blue."

This seesaw between her comments and my mirroring went on for about ten minutes. The supervising psychiatrist finally had enough and motioned for me to stop. He said, "Dr. Wicks, let's stop for a moment here." (I should have suspected that I was in for it when he referred to me as "doctor" since I hadn't finished the program of study yet.)

He then went on to say, "I don't think I have heard the nondirective approach used so consistently before." Still, not catching the inflection in his voice, I naively responded, "Thank you."

Finally, he added, "I did have one question though."

"Yes?" I replied, smiling like a happy puppy.

"When did you plan to begin the treatment?"

"What do you mean?" I asked.

He said: "Why didn't you ask her when she became depressed?"

(At this point, my fellow students seemed to lean away from me. They were staring at me with a look that said, "He's sinking. No sense in going down with him.") Finally, I replied defensively, "She's always been this depressed."

"Well then, when did she get worse?"

Adamantly defensive I said, "She's always been this bad."

To which he went on, "Well, why did she come into the clinic now?"

To which I parried, "Someone just told her that the clinic was here."

Undaunted, he went on, "Well, why did she decide to take her friend up on the suggestion that she go in at this time?"

To this I had no ready response, and after a moment or two of quiet he added, "Details, Doctor, details. If you want to just shoot the bull, go elsewhere. Once you find out the beginning of this problem, you will not only get a sense of the source of it but you will also indirectly instill hope. Because if there is a beginning to a problem, then by implication there is an end.

"We need to trace a problem to its source; look for what happened in the person's environment at the time of the problem's inception; see what the person was thinking and believing (perception); and, finally, see what the person has done or not done to deal with the issues at hand. Therapy is not magic; it is a behavioral science that is fired by the art of forming a relationship in which the person can *trust* and then providing useful information that can help the person make sense of the problem and structure a way to deal with it."

For religious individuals, this "trust" takes the form of "faith": faith not only in God but in the people in our environment who can support us as we face the suffering in our lives. Paradoxically and sadly, it is the painful moments in our lives that can be the strongest seeds of new spiritual strength and wisdom if we take the time, effort and risk to fully realize the source of our suffering and are willing to face it directly.

When painful memories are completely forgotten, they unconsciously retain a long-term depressive pull on our lives. Once remembered, on the other hand, they are brought out into the open air of an examined life. This helps us gain perspective and form the basis for growth and a better appreciation of our true identity with all the potential that such an understanding brings. If painful memories are not brought to the surface, they remain a fearful presence in a dark psychological and spiritual closet, the door to which we are frightened will burst open at any moment, leaving us naked, helpless and filled with a heavy sense of shame.

In our present age of abuse, terrorism, poverty and violence of all forms, both nurturing silence and terrible screams are the fabric of spirituality, of God's presence, of our being fully alive! *Acknowledged pain* is proof that we are alive. Our daily philosophy of life and faith must embrace *all* reality deeply if it is to survive and

71

flourish. To have a spirituality that is only comfortable when things are nice is fake. Moreover, to live with a Pollyannish attitude and mistake it for being the ground of hope is actually risky.

We can see this in Kathleen Norris's *Dakota* when she employs the approach to farming the land as a metaphor for hope based on true faith. In it she writes, "The Plains are not forgiving. Anything that is shallow—the easy optimism of a homesteader; the false hope that denies geography, climate, history; the tree whose roots don't reach ground water—will dry up and blow away."[12] To repeat the quote of Merton that opened this chapter: "True love and prayer are learned when love becomes impossible and the heart has turned to stone." In our desire to be a people of hope, we must not forget this reality. The dangers are too great if we do.

The journey during very difficult times is a movement toward or away from deep transformation. For instance, when adults realize that they were sexually abused as children, they feel lost and fearful, like abandoned children again. They get destabilized. They don't know who they are. They are fearful of who they may become if they continue to explore the reality of this early abuse, since for many years they formed their very selves around the denial of this abuse.

However, to move ahead in life, they need to face what happened to them, walk through the fear, depression and the sense of alienation from themselves and others, and *leap into the darkness* so that they can find out—in true freedom—who they really are and who they can be once the realities of their lives come to light. Once again, though, to accomplish this, they must trust. At first, this trust often takes the form of unrealistic expectations of friends and counselors. Such a transference is necessary so that they can chance becoming involved.

Then, after a while, they are let down because the supportive people in their lives cannot possibly meet all their unrealistic demands or live up to their images of perfection. But as their spiritual and psychological health is strengthened in these relationships, they begin to appreciate the fact that love is not proven by others meeting their *every* demand. Instead, it is the willingness on the part of the friend, therapist or spiritual companion to be patient and faithful, while still maintaining their personal freedom in the process. That is the true gift from God for the abused person that is offered through the support person.

I mention all this because the model of how an abused person leaves a false identity and moves through the darkness in trust to find a new identity is a reflection of what we all must go through in some way during the conversion process. All of us must, at some point, recognize how we have not trusted to look at ourselves and life directly enough so that we can see clearly, walk humbly and be faithful to our call to truly be alive, rather than be a puppet whose strings are pulled by unnecessary images, needs or accepted false identities from childhood. In other words, transformation and hearing the voice of silent hope require that we have enough trust *to be ordinary,* that is, to risk searching for and being our true selves. But as will be discussed in the next chapter, this too requires a special fund of courage and openness to transformation.

. . . .

FOR REFLECTION...

When problems arise in your life, do you place the "blame" outside of yourself or are you willing to trace the problem to its source?

How can such ownership and reflection on personal responsibility both free you from unnecessary guilt and at the same time help you move toward conversion of heart?

7. Simplicity and Ordinariness

→

Henry Thoreau warned us that our lives were being frittered away on details. His advice was, simplify, simplify, simplify. This recommendation to make life more elegant by removing unnecessary clutter and activities was— and still is—very compelling.

However, paring down our busy schedules while keeping our hearts complex is not an effective route to a life of simplicity. Our attitude is at the center of how we view life. It determines our behavior toward others, how we make daily decisions, and provides the basis for genuine simplicity.

When our attitude is not centered on what is truly important, we may see the possibility of the simple life. Yet, we will still view our harried schedules as proof that simplicity isn't possible for us. Even when we take steps to simplify, simplify, simplify, as Thoreau suggested, without a change in attitude, the problems of modern life will continue and eventually overwhelm our resolve. Thus, instead of there being new opportunities for peace in our more open schedule, almost without our knowing it, we will soon find other distractions and details filling the very space we just made available. Finally, when we realize what has happened, we will see this as proof that obviously there is no hope for change; given the demands on our life, we can't lead a gentle, passionate life.

The best physical analogy we have for this is dieting. People go on diets, lose water first so that they feel some sense of satisfaction, then follow an artificial program of eating that slims them down. Often, however, there is no deep attitude change. The result is inevitable: as soon as the diet is set aside, weight gain occurs, and, in many cases, the person may wind up even heavier than before! Attitude, not an artificial approach to food, is the cornerstone of achieving positive results. The same can be said of simplicity.

Simplicity relies first and foremost on an attitude of ordinariness. Ordinariness invites us to appreciate at a very basic level *who we are.* Then, given this identity, it calls us to discern *what we are to do in life*—not only in terms of a lifelong career or mission, but on a daily basis as well. Finally, it requires that we be aware of *how we are to live* based on knowing the crux of our simple philosophy of living. Who? What? How? The answers to three essential questions can foster greater simplicity in our lives—a very attractive proposal in these anxious, overwhelming times.

Who?: Ordinariness

Knowing who we are, our basic identity (what I referred to earlier as our "name" or "word"), is very freeing. Margaret Mitchell, who wrote *Gone with the Wind,* demonstrated her appreciation of this when she said that once we lose our reputation, we become truly free. Until then, we often rely not on the beautiful essence of our creation (in religious terms, who we are in the eyes of God), but instead make the world "a god" and let it determine our image and be the source of our "rewards" when we live up to its demands.

To appreciate this, it is good to look for a few minutes at our own life and see what pulls our strings. If people smile at us, we feel good. If they frown at us in the morning (even if it is from their having gastritis!), we may have a vague feeling that something is wrong all day. We wonder why they don't like us or whether we've done something wrong. Thus, time and energy are wasted on inaccurate thinking as we ruminate over it, trying to get a sense of what did or didn't happen and who was at fault.

A crazy example from my own life might help to further illustrate the point here—at least it helps me to remember how much energy supporting a false image takes since I tend toward pomposity when left on my own without a good spiritual baseline to follow. See how it might relate to your own life in some way.

A number of years ago, I got up in the morning after being out very, very late celebrating the night before. When I arose I looked in the mirror and thought, "Oh, what a fool I made of myself last night. I can barely look at myself today." Then as the rationalizations crept in, I thought, "Well, maybe I didn't behave so terribly." However, the truth embedded in my mirror seemed to look back at me and say, "No, you were right the first time; you made a complete fool out of yourself last night."

But then I thought, "Well, maybe I am blowing this out of proportion. No one probably even noticed that I was loud, monopolized the conversation and said stupid things to the people I was with." However, as I continued to stare at my face in the mirror, wondering if it was safe to shave, the other side of the truth quickly came to mind as if I were being censured by someone invisible in my head. I heard, "No sense in trying to play this down. You were so loud everyone heard your voice and proclamations; they probably wrote down your name on their napkins!"

Needless to say, by the time I got to work to see my patients that day, I was bereft of self-confidence. I felt that I had made a complete fool out of myself and there was no sense trying to excuse my behavior. As a matter of fact, I had a fantasy that the people who were coming to see me that day would look up and see my face and somehow know what a fool I had been. I had this terrible feeling that they would even jump up and say, "Wait a minute. Why am I coming to see you for help? You are obviously the one in need of real assistance!" Obviously the shame of the evening before was effectively working full time to contaminate the day.

After the day was complete, though, I was quite surprised at what seemed to transpire. I sat back in my chair and thought, "I don't believe it. This was one of the best days I've ever had in my clinical practice. The sessions seemed to be more meaningful. I handled the responses and challenges of the patients more sensitively. But why?"

Then, as I thought about it further, it hit me that the answer was *smallness*. By this, I mean *ordinariness* or what Thomas Merton would refer to as *the true self*. Because I had knocked myself off my imaginary pedestal by my embarrassing behavior the night before, I was able to be freer with my patients— something which is obviously very important for psychotherapy to be effective.

When people are in treatment, they are under a great deal of stress because they are being asked to let down their guard, to risk change, to touch upon sensitive parts of their lives and to exchange the expensive defenses they have been using for less expensive ones. All of this causes such stress that they will often challenge the therapist and attack her/his sense of well-being as a way of getting the focus off themselves. This is natural and to be expected. All of us do it in conversation when we feel stressed; and we experience this tendency as well during heated discussions and arguments.

Normally, when I experience this at the hands of another, it hurts because I am so filled with my own defenses and inflated self-image that, when they metaphorically swing at me, they can't miss. However, given the deflation of my image, I was so small, so reliant on the only thing that was left— my simple identity as a human being created by God— that they couldn't possibly hit me. The sensitive points they normally would have hit in a previous session were gone because I was truly aware of my own foibles and was able to accept them. I was not beating myself, but I was recognizing the fallacy of trying to put myself on a pedestal as a way of protecting myself. So, in the sessions that day, I could focus the attention back onto the patients, help them see their fear and anger and ease them toward uncovering a bit more of what was behind their negative emotions. I learned the hard way that the freedom that ordinariness and simplicity give to us when we have an insight into our own defensiveness also can turn out to be a gift to others as well.

I was able on another occasion to appreciate the gift of ordinariness when I heard the story of a contemporary figure who was so deeply spiritual that he could only be his ordinary self. His name is Archbishop Desmond Tutu. A colleague of mine, who once hosted a visit by the Archbishop, related a brief story that made a strong point of how wonderfully helpful the gift of ordinariness can be to the world.

He said that Desmond Tutu was visiting his seminary and giving a talk to the seminarians gathered before him. Halfway through the presentation, one of the seminarians seated next to the dean said, "You know, Desmond Tutu is truly a holy man."

The dean was surprised by such an overarching evaluation and naturally inquired, "How do you know this?" (The seminarian should have known better than to make such a broad statement to a theological dean and expect to get away with it without being challenged!) However, the seminarian was not in the least flustered by the demand for elaboration. He didn't blink but merely replied: "I know that Desmond Tutu is a holy man because when I am with Desmond Tutu, *I feel holy.*"

It is important then to recognize the following spiritual truth: An attitude of ordinariness, which is a key source of simplicity, is a gift of freedom not only to ourselves but also to others who encounter us when we are in this open, gentle place. I guess that this shouldn't be too surprising to us, though. For isn't it true that any real grace that we embrace fully for ourselves is one that naturally winds up being shared with others, almost without our even having to think about it?

What?: Our Mission in Life

When we know who we are (ordinariness), it is easier to determine what we should do, both in daily encounters and in life in general. The "what" does not refer to our job or activity. It speaks of the main contribution we offer others.

Several years ago, I thought that I might best consider a career change. My sense was that I was getting stagnant. Living just outside of Washington, D.C., I noted ample opportunities to be of support to the country through a position in government. I also considered the possibility of becoming president of a small college. The thoughts about such changes ran through my head.

As I was thinking about this, an article appearing in *America* magazine listed key books in spirituality twenty-five years ago as well as those that were on that same list now. I made the new top ten list by the skin of my teeth—you guessed it, number ten!

In the article there were also a few lines about me. Thus, when I had a chance to speak with the author of the piece, I teased, "Whew. It was touch and go there. I am glad I made number ten." I also thanked him for including a few lines here and there about my contribution. To this, he said something that surprised me, "You know, Bob, there are a lot of people who write good books on spirituality. What they write is very helpful, but then that's it. You, on the other hand, are a *consistent* presence in the field through your integration of psychology and spirituality."

After I got off the phone, I saw this comment as an indication that my "what" really was the integration of psychology and spirituality. I didn't need to change fields to refresh myself; I needed to go *deeper*. I needed to see anew how this integration was present in all phases of my life: teaching, clinical work, interactions with family and friends, reflection...even my passing encounters with people in stores and hallways. I was now clear once again on the "what"—that is, my mission at this phase of my life.

One of the questions that all of us need to ask at various points in life to help us stay on the most rewarding spiritual road possible is this: What is the *charism,* gift or theme of our lives that we bring to all situations? This question is part of the process of solidifying simplicity of attitude and heart.

How?: Our Philosophy of Life

Knowing our real "word" or "name" (the "who") before God is an important aspect of firming up our identity so that we can weather the storms of loss, discouragement, interpersonal discord and other attacks on our image as a person. As was just noted, knowing our mission or *charism* in life (the "what") also helps us to discern the overriding activity with which we are meant to gift life. The final piece of this trio is having a philosophy of life that can help us determine our way of perceiving and interacting with the world. This is the "how" of our life.

For me, in the work that I do, I find that it is easy to be destabilized when catapulted into the turmoil of other people's worlds. As a result, I realize that I need not only a clear sense of who I am and what my gifts are, but also I need to know what guiding principle I am using in interacting with life, given my identity and gifts.

With this realization, I started writing a philosophy that was too long at first. I also noticed that I had either a tendency to be too general or much, much too specific. Finally, I settled on a one-liner:

Be clear, and be not afraid, for you are loved by God.

Using this theme, I realized how I valued each part of this one simple sentence that I had composed and saw how one piece would set the stage for the next part to follow:

Be clear: I felt that the truth would indeed set me free. I also believed that since I am psychodynamic in orientation (that is, I believe that the unconscious can impact conscious daily life), it is important to see how the past clouds my view of reality in the present. I am also cognitive (I see how beliefs affect thinking and, in turn, how my thought process— especially erroneous thinking— will impact whether I am depressed or not), so I want to test to see the accuracy of another's beliefs about life.

Be not afraid: Fear traps me and causes my life to become very narrow. Uncovering and discovering what makes me anxious and afraid can help me see where I waste a great deal of energy on defense and retreat— energy that could be spent on enjoying life and being creative.

For you are loved by God: Being clear is essential and being afraid is unnecessary when I feel loved. And the deepest love— even more profound than self-love— is a sense that God loves me, that I am one with the universe.

With this philosophy, then, I have a theme in life that I can return to again and again when feeling lost or challenged. Developing or formulating greater clarity toward the personal philosophy that we want guiding us takes some time and reflection. But the challenge to do so, to take a one-liner and test it out in life, is an essential part of having an attitude of simplicity and knowing who we are as *extra-ordinary* persons walking this earth at this time.

So, simplicity and ordinariness are not gifts that come of just making our outward life circumstances small— though certainly simplifying our life is a wonderful step. Instead, simplicity is primarily grown in the interior soul. It is an outgrowth of our having clarity and warm acceptance of an identity, a mission and a philosophy of life that are life-giving. Moreover, such simplicity helps us see more quickly those ways in which we either welcome or reject the love around us, which is the topic to be discussed next.

. . . .

FOR REFLECTION...

Who are you? Do you know your true name?

Why is becoming "ordinary" so difficult a process?

How would you describe the connections among ordinariness, simplicity and true inner freedom? What role do they play or would you like them to play in your life?

Describe those times when you feel most free.

Spend some time developing a one-sentence theme that has the potential to guide you toward true (inner) simplicity, clarity and peace.

8. Hearing the Soft Whisper
of Love

→

Leaving for work that morning, I had a sense that it was going to snow. The sky was foreboding and the temperature seemed just cold enough. However, since I enjoy the little dramas of life, I tend to overpredict such things.

By midmorning, though, I knew that this time I was right. The flakes, huge ones, started to fall. From where I sat in the office, the effect outside my window was beautiful. The large, dark spruces in the distance seemed happy to be dressed lightly in white. Even the grumpy old oaks immediately outside my window were softened by the dusting of snow.

While I was seeing patients early in the day, slowly, large flakes alighted on the ones before them. They landed so quietly that I didn't realize that over one foot of snow had already fallen with the prospect of more to come. By late afternoon I had moved from "Ah, isn't it beautiful?" to "Oh no! How the heck am I ever going to get out of here?"

During one of my breaks, the phone rang. It was my last patient, a very fine lawyer from town. She was psychologically healthy, quite assertive, very intelligent and really seeing me only to help her gain clarity around a job change as well as to increase self-awareness.

After I got on the line she said: "Given the weather, I think I'll cancel today's session."

Instead of a sensible reaction on my part, this was the first thing that struck me: "Oh sure, I'm stuck here and have to trek all the way home later tonight, but you don't want to bother yourself about trying to get in."

I have a standard policy that patients need to cancel twenty-four hours prior to a scheduled session or they get charged. If I had been thinking clearly, however, I would have realized that surely the weather provided mitigating circumstances. However, since I was in such a bad mood, I found myself saying, "Well the decision is up to you."

She picked up something in my voice and said with an incredulous tone in her voice, "You are not going to charge me are you?" I responded in an unpleasant voice, "You're darn right I am."

Hearing this she said, "Well, all right, then, I'm coming in tonight!" and then abruptly hung up.

After getting off the phone, I thought, "What a fool I am! Of course she had a good reason to skip. If I had any sense at all I, myself, would cancel the rest of my hours and go home now." Then I reflected, "Now she is going to come in here as angry as ever (which I clearly deserved, given my ridiculous behavior)." And, reflecting on what I thought I would confront, I felt that I would be willing now to pay *her* not to come in! But I was to be totally surprised by what happened.

Instead of coming in angry, she had a somewhat triumphant look on her face as she sat down across from me. As soon as she was in the chair, she said with a big smile, "You were angry at me when I told you that I was going to cancel; you really got upset when I expected not to have to pay for the session, didn't you?"

Knowing that honesty is the best policy, I responded, "Well, to be honest, I wasn't angry...actually I was furious."

"Aha, I thought so," she said, still smiling.

I couldn't delay my question any longer and said: "But why are you smiling, given my ridiculous behavior?"

She said, "Because you let your guard down and I could see how you *really* felt. It was the first time that you had gotten angry at me in therapy. To see your veneer crack made me sense that I was finally getting an authentic response."

After about fifteen or twenty seconds of silence (although in therapy it always seems longer), her comment had a chance to sink in with me and I said, "You know, when I have said positive things to you in the past, you did not respond with as much animation as you just have. I do apologize for my being short with you on the phone and my rigid stance regarding cancellation. It was totally uncalled for. However, the question I am left with at this point is, why do you hear praise in a whisper and negative things as thunder? Why is the positive I share with you not really important or real, and the negative more authentic?"

With this question hanging in the air before us, we spent the rest of the session building an answer that showed how criticism in her life seemed more real than praise. We explored why encouragement seemed less alive or valued than the negative comments she received.

Rejection or minimization of praise and hypersensitivity to criticism are real problems for many of us. Because of them, our self-esteem suffers. Then, because of low self-esteem, a negative cycle begins and we start to minimize praise and exaggerate criticism. We also wind up chasing after persons who reject us in an effort to win them over, believing that somehow this will help increase self-value. Paradoxically, there is also a failure to appreciate the nurturing elements that are already in one's surroundings.

In other words, we are often encircled by unrecognized and unaccepted love and complain that it isn't there! The reason for this may be that we can't believe that people love (respect, have faith in, etc.) us or we demand that love be shown in specific ways or we deem them as really not signs of love.

In my years of supervising faculty and students, I have often found this to be a problem. Some people feel that unless you agree with their perceptions and act accordingly, you don't care for them or believe in their overall abilities. The truth is that the most loving thing one can often do is not to go along with people when they are wrong in their perceptions because it will only end in their getting into more trouble. This in no way, however, is to be equated with a lack of respect or love for them.

To change this unfortunate pattern we need to reconceptualize our ideas of love and increase our sensitivity to the praise and positive feedback we do get and often (because of habit) minimize or set aside. The change in the way that we view "love" requires that we begin to look at *every* thing and event that is positive in our lives and welcome each and every one with open arms.

Warmth and love are in the smile of a grocery clerk and the rising of the morning sun. They are in an enjoyable phone call and in a serious discussion that is thought-provoking. They are in a cup of coffee and a hot bagel enjoyed in the early afternoon. Warmth and love are reflected in the manifestation of *all* goodness that we experience in life.

Some would say, "Oh, you're watering down the intense experience of love. You are like the soap companies that play love songs during their ads to make you think that love means washing your face with their soap!" No, I don't want to dilute the purity and unique experience of love for a special person or cause. What I do want to do, however, is to raise the level of consciousness in myself and others to the loving gifts of life that we either ignore, play down or take for granted.

This concept is important to appreciate because things and events that are positive experiences help us face the challenges in life. Likewise, positive feedback (praise) also strengthens us for the difficult times and critical comments of others. Yet, we often react to such support from others by diminishing the importance of the statements. We can see this when people get an evaluation from a supervisor. It is as though they are in a trance during the positive feedback, waiting only to wake up when the constructive criticism is brought to the fore.

The positive assets of a person are just as important as the areas that need improvement— maybe even more so. It is the positive traits that will eventually need to be mobilized so that people can feel better. If the focus in psychotherapy and spiritual guidance is only on the negative, then the people being guided can't help themselves; they need to be pulled up solely through the efforts of those trying to support them in their search for clarity and under-standing. On the other hand, if the positive can be the focus for both parties, it is then possible through a *joint* effort to address the liabilities that the person has brought to the therapy. The same can be said of life in general. The more we are aware of our own talents, the more we can strengthen and employ them to offset or correct our faults.

Thus, every effort needs to be taken to become more aware of the positive in our environment, whether it is something impersonal (weather, food) or relational (a compliment). In doing this, the whisper of praise and the presence of goodness in our environment can be received more readily on a daily basis. The strength and bal-ance that such an awareness will provide will be amazing. Further-more, our efforts in this regard will help us keep perspective in life.

. . . .

FOR REFLECTION...

Where and from whom do you hear your words of encourage-ment? Why do those words encourage you?

How and when do you become a source of encouragement for others? When and why do you find it difficult to offer an encouraging word?

How have you personally benefited from both positive and negative feedback? Why are both essential for your spiritual and psychological well-being?

9. Spiritual Freedom

→

The great composer Vladimir Horowitz once said, "The piano is the easiest instrument to play but the hardest instrument to play well."[13] I think that the same can be said of life.

It is very easy to exist, to go along with others and to allow hidden values to drive us in a direction that makes us unhappy. There is an old rabbinical saying that states, "Do not limit your children to your own learning for they have been born in another age." A saying such as this has as much relevance for us as it does for our children.

While we must be open to the beautiful traditions of our parents and those who came before us, we must at the same time be careful not to worship the past (traditionalism). Instead, being open to what is creative and good is essential—even when it seems to be impossible.

As was mentioned in an earlier chapter, in the Christian New Testament we read Paul's admission to the Romans (7:15): "I cannot understand my own behavior. I fail to carry out the things I must do, and I find myself doing the very things I hate." This disclosure of an experience of discouragement on his part is wonderful, for it shows that he knows and admits that he is stuck.

Such an awareness is a beginning, but many of us close ourselves off to seeing our resistance to the truth about ourselves. And those of us who proclaim to be in the business of helping others discover the truth about themselves and the way they face the world (i.e., counselors, spiritual directors...) are certainly not exempt from such blindness.

I remember feeling quite low one Christmas Eve. My daughter was not coming home for Christmas, but had decided instead to stay in Florida and take a post-Christmas vacation up in Ohio with her boyfriend's family. After thinking about it, I realized that it wasn't her absence on Christmas that bothered me, but a final recognition that she no longer would be popping in during holidays or on breaks because she lived far away. She wasn't in the next town or even the next state. When I related this to a friend, she said, "Bob, that's what they call empty-nest syndrome." To this I made a face and said, "Cathy, I am a psychologist. I don't get empty-nest syndrome!"

People can go all through life denying the truth and hiding from beliefs they unconsciously hold. When we do this, however, we cut our chances of changing to near zero. We may even follow a way of thinking and feeling about ourselves that is totally wrong, but that we swallowed when we were too young to understand what we were being asked to accept. Such is the basis of an insightful under-standing of human development. During therapy, the goal is to have the person see what he or she has taken into his or her belief system and see its distorting impact on self-awareness and relation-ships with others (including God in prayer) and how this can be altered once the truth surfaces.

A physician who came to see me many years ago complained that his parents always treated him like a little child. In one session he whined, "Why do they do that?"

Since our relationship was fairly well cemented and he was used to me teasing him to make a point, I whined in return, "I can't imagine why they would treat you like a child."

To this he laughed and said, "I don't sound that bad, do I?" We then spent the rest of the session looking at the negative thoughts and beliefs he had about himself when he was tired, felt taken advantage of by others or had failed at something. For him and for all of us, it is during those periods that negative self-perceptions surface and we can see what we truly believe about ourselves though we might, in most other instances, protest to the contrary.

Self-awareness helps us to look at negative self-perceptions directly and confront them. It also helps us to explore psychological suffering in order to understand patterns in our life that can be changed.

If we use a rock falling on our head as a metaphor for our suffering, the most common reactions that the majority of people would have to the situation are as follows:

— They feel it is a mistake that the rock fell on them, so they don't think about it any further until it falls on them again;

— They say, "Life is like that; suffering is a part of it," so they don't do anything about it.

— There is a recognition that this suffering is undesirable, but they don't admit that they have a role in avoiding it or making it less, so they just project the blame onto others, complain and say things will be better when the world (friends, family, job conditions, society, their church...) changes;

— They protest such suffering and take steps to make the rocks smaller so that when they fall, they won't hurt as much.

The answer instead is to MOVE YOUR HEAD! By this I mean see what role we have in creating or exacerbating a situation that we don't like. See what beliefs we hold that are causing us suffering.

For example, adults like the physician noted above come to see me and tell me that their parents don't treat them like adults. I examine them with their expectations that their parents treat them otherwise. The point I try to make with them is this: We can't change our parents, but we can change our expectations for them and our belief that our own sense of adulthood *depends* on their and other people's perceptions of us. Part of the task of adolescence and young adulthood is to lessen reliance on others to serve as mirrors of our self-esteem. That is why quiet time and prayer are essential. In meditation, we allow our self-doubts and our dependence on others for approval to rise to the surface. We then place ourselves before a loving God and seek to find and reinforce in ourselves the beautiful essence of who we are *independent of the views of others or even our own opinion of ourselves based on what we can do rather than who we are.*

In counseling others, we witness to the truth of a situation rather than confront a person who is resisting the truth or reluctant to change; if you do this you will lose, because facing resistance head on produces only more resistance to change. Instead, we go around the resistance and, rather than confronting the person, we present the realities that the person has shared with us and let these realities confront the person. For instance, we say, "Here is what you've been saying and doing. These are the results of your thoughts and actions. What do you think of this pattern?"

A spirit of openness thus helps us to realize that we are always bound at some level and that we need to be intrigued and innervated by the mystery of this resistance rather than discouraged by it. We need to see our resistance clearly so that truth and self-knowledge can help us "move our heads" rather than keep them where the rocks can fall on them. In other words, we need to examine our own resistance to profitable change.

The first step in doing this is to embrace the passion of truth as we look at behaviors that seem to be holding us back. When we are honest with ourselves in reflection (without picking on ourselves inordinately, which will only cause us to avoid such self-awareness processes from occurring), pray with a real desire to be naked before God and try to be as honest and vulnerable as possible with a mentor, counselor or spiritual guide, then the seeds of change and a melting of our resistance can become possible in mysterious ways. An example from my own life may shed some light on this process.

For years I felt that I drank too much. I would have several drinks almost every evening after work. When I went out to dinner, I also would never pass up the chance for a few scotches and/or glasses of wine. At times I would recognize that alcohol was playing an inordinately important role in my life; it had become sort of an idol. I never denied that I was drinking too much, but little changed in my pattern. It provided rewards— the instant gratification of feeling relaxed, for instance— and I played down what it was costing me and those who had to deal with me when I drank.

Despite my level of denial and my resistance to change, I continued to speak with my spiritual director about it, prayed over it and journaled about it. I thought that a change was important, but I wasn't sure how this would come about since the problem wasn't bad enough for me to confront myself with the truth— or, for that matter, have someone else do it.

Then an interesting thing happened. I was expecting an extended visit from a friend who was a recovering alcoholic. My wife reminded me of his situation and recommended that I not drink in his presence since he was still uncomfortable around people drinking. I agreed and even stopped a few days early because I'd had too much to drink and had a hangover two days prior to his visit.

After he left, I didn't start drinking again that week...that month...that year. I just stopped. When people asked me about it, I was puzzled. They said, "Do you miss it?" I replied, "Not intensely, but I do miss having a few, particularly after a long hard day or on the weekends."

Some asked: "Do you feel tempted when you are around people drinking?" My response was and is "No. I enjoy serving those who drink sensibly and enjoy it without it being a health problem for them." The whole business was so strange that I began to reflect on my long resistance to change and where I was with this previous problem now. The image that came to mind in reflection and chatting about it with others was that of "a garden."

I always had the sense that the world was like a garden filled with many wonderful things— people, walks in the country, quiet time in an old church, a leisurely meal with a friend...the list was endless. In the case of drinking however, I had chosen only one of the flowers, and because of it I was unable to enjoy the rest of the garden.

I realized that, on another level, the garden of life was the part of God that I could see. I remembered Jesus' question about the possibility of loving a God whom we could not see if we didn't love our brothers and sisters, whom we could see. The world's beauty was a reflection of and a path to God. However, if I centered only on one small part of the garden, not only would I miss the beauty of everything else, but I would also be replacing God with this idol.

Being present to the entire garden, though, took some adjustment. I wasn't used to it. Releasing this idol meant that I was often left bored and without peace. I realized how searchers for God in the fourth-century deserts of Persia and northern Africa were confronted with *acedia* (spiritual boredom).

I needed to sit in the emptiness at times and not rush back to alcohol or other types of addictions (work, the search for power or acceptance, etc.). Instead, I had to realize that this period of quiet in my life was a darkness that would really bring new light if I allowed myself to learn from it. I needed, once again, to be *intrigued by my resistances to change* and to simply flow with the beauty of life, to live with a sense of simplicity and hope. I needed to seek with a sense of passion and "spiritual curiosity" the basic Truth of life which, of course, relies on sound, nonjudgmental self-awareness.

. . . .

FOR REFLECTION...

What is your philosophy or theology of suffering? (If you do not have either a philosophy or theology of suffering, explore and develop your thoughts about suffering, why and how it exists, and whether you believe there is any value that can come out of it.)

What aspects of your life do you think could benefit from change? What changes have you long resisted making? What do you think are the sources of these resistances to change in yourself and what can you do to overcome them?

10. Truth, Self-Knowledge...Choice

→

Existentialist philosopher Karl Jaspers stated one of the most basic challenges of life when he said, "What makes us afraid is our great freedom in the face of the emptiness that has still to be filled."[14] Clarity about this reality is something most of us want to avoid a good deal of the time. What this reality does is put us on notice that we *do* have choices and we constantly *make* choices whether we admit or know it. Each of our choices has consequences. Each of our decisions leads us in a particular direction and moves us away from other possibilities.

Awareness of this can be frightening and, once again, raise our resistance to seeing it because we will then have to take responsibility for choosing or not choosing some direction. It is always easier to point outward than it is to see inward so that we can claim our role and responsibilities in life. That is why fantasy is so alluring. In fantasy, we use up all of our energy thinking, "What if?" In the more mature activity of dreaming, we still ask, "What if?" but we also reserve enough energy to act on those ideas and hopes we have allowed to rise in our hearts. To move from being a fantasy person to a dreamer who participates in life—rather than one who is merely a spectator to other people's spiritual adventures in living—takes courage and a willingness to see realities as they truly are. The following encounter may illustrate what this participation in life involves.

Once a person came in to see me complaining of her tendency toward impulsiveness. When I asked her for an example, she told me that recently she had told off her boyfriend and now they were on the outs. "I didn't think before I spoke. I just lashed out and now we don't talk to each other anymore. We could have worked it out if only I had not verbally blasted him."

"Well, what exactly did he do that made you so angry?" I asked.

"I found out that he had gone out behind my back with my best friend."

"Let me see if I have this right. He actually dated your *best* friend without your knowing it?" (I stated this with emphasis to encourage her to get back in touch with what she felt at the time.)

"Yes, he did." (She now was getting angry with him again.)

"Well, were you wild at this when you heard about it?"

"You better believe it!"

"Well, what did you do?"

"I picked up the phone and called him."

"What did you say to him?"

With great energy, she then related how she told him off, using very "colorful" language. (My thought at the time was: "I've never heard those words put together like that.")

After she finished her story, I said, "Then did you slam down the phone on him?"

"I did!" she said triumphantly.

I replied, "Well, you told him off, didn't you? I'll bet it was good to get that off your chest. I'm sure you felt relieved to have let him know how you felt."

"Yes, it was good to let it out," she replied. But after that, we never spoke again."

At that point I took off my glasses, paused and said, "Well, we really can't have it both ways in life. Either we have the pleasure of letting out steam whenever and wherever we want and take the consequences of such actions, or we think through our actions and reflect before acting. We may still want to cut off a relationship with someone who has been deceitful, but it will be *our* choice and not the result of impulse and temporary emotion. It sounds like you want to reclaim your ability to make a choice. However, the first step in doing this is to recognize that there is a choice. We are already opting for one of the selections possible which, as in any choice, has both good and unfortunate consequences."

Choice and Resistance

We need to examine what we want to do, how we want to do it, and what the possible results of our actions will be. Truth offers freedom and possibility when we honestly look at ourselves and start with good self-knowledge; of course it isn't ever easy.

We often face the truth about ourselves with hostility and fear though we hide this reality— even from ourselves. We hide hostility toward the truth under the guise of "annoyance," and we refer to our fear as "caution" or "natural hesitation." Plain truth is often ridiculed as simplistic, and we avoid taking the next step because "it just won't do any good."

Jesus indicated that people preferred the darkness to the light, and this is true of us all more often than we care to admit. Even when challenged by friends to change or grow, we smile patiently and say something to the effect: "If you only knew...." "If you had only been through what I have...." Or, "Once you get to be my age...." (This, of course, is impossible because when we *do* she or he will still be older!) Or, another popular response to fend off others is, "It's easy for you to say...."

Overcoming resistances to the truth, self-knowledge, and the responsibility we have to choose our destiny can be achieved by paying a little attention each day to our lives. Pacing ourselves, forming a good relationship (friendship actually) with ourselves, increasing our curiosity about our ways of facing the day and fostering our own self-esteem so that we can embrace the unpleasant without giving up our self-confidence and identity in the process—all of these can help us melt resistance to the truth.

In counseling others, *pacing* is essential. This delicate balancing act requires the need to move fast enough in the treatment so that the person is not bored, yet not so fast that the person is caused undue anxiety. There's an old, unpleasant but true maxim that warns, "You shouldn't try to teach a pig to sing. It frustrates the teacher and irritates the hell out of the pig!"

Pacing is equally important with ourselves. We must be honest in our movement toward progress. There are times when we state that we want to change something and call it "trying," but either we really believe that it is impossible or we have no intention of following through. However, taking small steps in the direction we want to go is possible if we set reasonable goals and then meet them.

Often with people I hear the comment, "I've been going in the wrong direction so long, what good would change do for me now?" The image that I offer them in return is of someone lost in the forest. Turning around and taking the first outward step once you see the way you need to go provides an immediate sense of relief and hope.

Having a good relationship with ourselves is also essential to overcoming resistance to change or seeing the truth about ourselves. In counseling, a foundation for helping people make progress is the relationship between the counselor and the client. If he or she has a high degree of trust in the helper, the person seeking assistance is more willing to take a risk than if there is little confidence in the person offering guidance.

Once again, the same is true with respect to our relationship with ourselves. It is often easier to trust others than ourselves, so we need to work even harder on self-appreciation. When we trust in our own goodness and value and are able to articulate clearly the gifts that we have been given in which others take joy, then we will be more apt to risk change and to see the truth about ourselves, even if it may seem negative at the time.

That is why *fostering self-esteem* is so important. When we have sound self-confidence, we can toughen our psychological skins to criticisms from others as well as to self-criticism so that we can admit our foibles, tease ourselves about them, learn from them and keep going.

Once, when a supervisor of mine was listening to me present a case in a way that showed that I was self-conscious about all of my errors, he said, "You seem to be very sensitive about making many poor interventions, but that is what occurs for new counselors. It may help to know that experienced counselors probably make the same number of errors in a session. However, there are two differences between them and new therapists such as yourself."

I was intrigued so I asked, "What are the differences?"

He said, "The mistakes are hopefully more sophisticated and subtle. And the experienced therapist is less judgmental with him/herself, so learning rather than self-condemnation is at the heart of the process."

Curiosity is also an essential part of overcoming our hesitancy to seeing ourselves clearly. In therapy we try to intrigue people with their behavior, feelings, thoughts and beliefs. Essentially what we are doing is trying to get them to drop their resistance to looking at their resistance!

We can use this same model with respect to self-understanding. Rather than picking on or excusing ourselves when we make a mistake, fail, have an unpleasant interaction or do something foolish, we need to look at ourselves with a sense of fascination. In this way, we see ourselves as mysteries to unravel and enjoy rather than as offenders to be condemned or defended at all cost.

Truth, self-knowledge and choice are all part of uncovering our resistances to seeing clearly. Together, they form the foundation of a life filled with clarity, depth and meaning. When we see the purpose and goals of our lives as clearly as we can, then flowing through life rather than drifting or compulsively being driven by forces we can't fathom becomes possible. Also, with a deep desire for self-awareness, the "silent rules" that have long been running our lives from within can be surfaced, gently and carefully examined, and changed if they no longer offer us life. As a matter of fact, since this is an important topic in itself, we will look at the topic of our "silent rules" next.

. . . .

FOR REFLECTION...

Does the statement, "We all learn by our mistakes" sound to you like a truism or a "cop-out"?

What does self-knowledge have to do with making choices?

Why and how do you place obstacles in your own path toward honest self-knowledge?

11. Uncovering Our Own "Silent Rules"

→

Taking risks is an essential part of living a psychologically and spiritually passionate and healthy life. This doesn't mean acting rashly and impulsively (which ironically is often done by some of us after a lengthy period of fearful nonaction). Risk means being open to opportunities after a disciplined discernment about the options available and a willingness to try the one that seems best.

The process of taking risks is generally examined within the realm of choosing a new path or undertaking. For instance, when risk taking comes up in sessions with people in counseling or mentoring, it usually takes the form of a question about whether to take a new job, move in a new direction, and so forth.

However, risk also impacts how we perceive who and what is *already* within our lives. Risk allows us to look at the rules that we have set up for ourselves, to see if they make sense and help us to be more integrated, or if they are leading us astray. As people who are free to take risks, we need to ask whether our rules give structure where there may have been chaos, provide guidance where there is a lack of direction, or hamper us—because of unnecessary fear and ignorance.

Rules upon which we do not reflect can take on a life and power of their own. Even though we, our parents, culture or an immature understanding of religion may have formed them, as time goes on, we may view them as if they came down from God: a new set of commandments! This is dangerous to our spiritual and psychological health because unconscious regulations that are never examined and are allowed to go unchecked may easily produce burnout and frustration.

In my sessions with others, I question them further about the philosophy that prompts them to say, "I can't do that" or "I should do that." This is done so that they can review their rules and underlying philosophies anew to see if they are viewing themselves, their duties and the world in a way that is spiritually and psychologically sound at this point in their development. On the contrary, they may discover that their rules and philosophies are unduly hampering them. A couple of illustrations may point out more clearly what I mean in this regard.

Once a Catholic religious sister came to see me because she was on the edge of burnout. I could see in her eyes when she came in that both her body and soul were tired. She was working harder and harder to accomplish less and less. Her schedule seemed to be a seamless garment of tasks to do and people to please.

In her history, she related that, for the past two years, every weekend she would leave the convent and go home to take care of her dad. During the week, she would teach chemistry to high school students. She had done this for twenty-six years.

First, I questioned her about her visits to her father. It seemed that she went there every weekend because she felt that he could die at any time, although he had been in a fragile state for over six months.

When she discussed teaching, she said that she felt really burned out but also felt that she had no choice. In her words: "The community needs me to continue teaching. Besides, we are a teaching community."

As the session proceeded, I found her to be a very talented person: quite psychologically healthy, very caring and compassionate and possessing a deep, spiritual passion. I was taken with her giftedness but also simultaneously struck by the "invisible rules" that she had set out for herself. She had cornered herself with no option for escape.

I was concerned that if she continued at this pace, she would physically and emotionally break down. When a person has what we call an "archaic superego," he or she is crushed by a rigid conscience. Rather than having an ego healthy enough to accept one's self as is and realizing that limits as well as the need to grow are natural for us all, such a person will find him-or herself under stress all the time, trying to live up to a long list of "shoulds."

As I sat there I thought, what should I do? I didn't feel that she and her religious congregation needed to spend money on a year's worth of therapy. It would have helped her gain greater self-understanding in many areas of her life, but I thought that focusing on just the present complaint would be fine for now. She could decide on the wisdom of any broader therapy later.

I also felt that I could use the positive transference she had toward me to make some quick changes in the style of her behavior. She had known some previous patients of mine and read a few of my books, so she trusted that I would steer her in a right direction. However, her style was a bit more ingrained than I thought; as you will see, it required a bit of an additional "push," shall we say.

Dealing first with the more pressing need for some time off in her schedule, I told her that she needed to start taking off one weekend per month from visiting her father so that she could get some rest and leisure time with friends. I told her that by the time she came in for her next visit with me, she should arrange her first visit to a friend so that she could get out of the convent and arrange for someone else to be with her father.

She surprised me with a quick, "Oh, I couldn't do that." I responded (my little push) by saying, "Well, then, let me talk to you a little about hospitalization for down the road."

She inquired quickly: "Hospitalization?"

"Now, I know what you may think of hospitals, but we have many fine institutions today, and I am sure that we can find one that you would find comfortable when the time comes."

"You think I am that bad?"

"Oh, yes, if you won't let yourself take time off or follow the rest of the prescription for dealing with this delicate state in your life and wish to be the doctor, the snowball that is rushing down the hill will only pick up additional speed. There's an old saying from an antifreeze commercial: 'You can pay me now a little bit to save the engine; or you can pay me later a lot to replace the whole mechanical system.' "

She paused and then said, "Well, I guess my father will be all right for one weekend. It's silly of me to think that he might die when I'm not there."

I wanted to deal with this type of thinking right away, while I had it in front of me. I also wanted her to avoid feeling terribly guilty if her father should die while she was away, so I said, "No, he may well die while you are away, so let's face that fact right now. He also may die when you are here, when you are teaching, when you are sleeping. You need to face this reality directly now. Otherwise, you are setting yourself up to feel unnecessary guilt when he does die."

She looked at me and said, "You know, I never thought about it that way. He could die when I am at school or at the supermarket. I just feel so responsible."

"By next session, then, come up with a plan to take off a weekend a month for the next three months. The plan should include spending time with a friend who does not live in the convent where you are living, so that you can get a change. Do you have somebody like that to visit?"

"Yes, I do," she said.

"Good. It is now February, so I also want you to look at a time when you can take a longer period away on some sort of break or holiday. Have that plan ready as well."

She made a face at that point so I said, "Stop with the faces. I am not asking you to go to the Taj Mahal—just to plan a bit of time off somewhere. It needs to be planned, however, so that you don't wind up at home for the whole time. Also, let me know how you expect to let your father and the rest of your family know about these plans so that we can role play the exchanges.

"Finally, I'd like you to talk to the personnel director in your religious congregation who is responsible for assignments. You act like you have been teaching for two years. If I remember right, it is twenty-six years; many people who have taught that long are retired. So, I'd like you to explore (she was giving me faces again), just *explore* possibilities other than teaching.

"If you wish me to speak with her and feel comfortable with my offering some of my reflections, then have her call me. If you would like to handle it all on your own, that is fine, too. But you obviously need a change. Just a weekend or two off won't alleviate the pattern you are in. You are entering the next phase of your life, and to greet it, you must be willing to welcome it on a number of levels—psychological, spiritual and vocational. Nothing has to be done overnight. But we need to be open to exploring possibilities."

I paused and held my breath. She looked at me and responded, "I guess I know you are right. I just didn't want to face it. I'll do what you say."

In the next session, she said that her father surprised her by saying he was pleased she was going to take some time away. Her brother had also agreed to stop in on the weekends that she would be away. She hadn't made an appointment with the personnel director for the congregation, so I gave her a little nudge to do this as well as to plan a summer holiday.

The meeting with the personnel board went well. The director said that a request for change after twenty-six years was reasonable. She also felt that Sister's gifts could be used elsewhere and suggested that they meet again.

By the third session, Sister had planned a vacation at the shore with a friend. Though it would be done very economically and was far from elaborate, she was overjoyed with the idea of it.

On the fifth visit, she surprised me with her opening gambit, "I hope you won't be offended. I really do enjoy speaking with you and you have been helpful."

I said, "But...?"

"But I feel better now that I have taken a weekend off. I have planned several more as well as a little summer vacation. It looks like I won't be teaching chem next year. Well, I feel all right. I just don't know what to talk with you about."

I laughed. She laughed. We realized that she had broken the logjam and was well on the road to claiming the next phase of her life. All she needed was a little Wicks' "push."

We often need someone to give us the permission to do what is reasonable: to move away from the list of rules that we have set up for ourselves so that we can explore other ways of living our lives. Not only can therapy and spiritual guidance help in this regard, but so can speaking with our friends and even thinking things through ourselves. The simple dictum, "What are the fruits?" will help us. If the fruits of our rules are anxiety and stress, we have to ask if the rules that we have made up are really good ones. Likewise, we have to be careful that the *rules* we have made don't become somehow spiritualized into rules that *God* has given us. We just don't know that much to make such overarching rules. We need help for such guiding principles, and that is why a community of friends and a philosophy of living that is open to new information and change are necessary; with their help, we can greet each different phase of life in a healthier way.

The same can be said of the rules we make for others. Once, when I was in another country working with priests, I asked one of them if he was under a good deal of stress. In response he quipped, "No. But I think I'm a carrier!"

Too often, when we put unreasonable expectations on people, they feel stressful and we do as well. The baselines we have for people may actually seem quite reasonable from the perspective of our value systems. However, to expect specific people in our lives to meet those guidelines is a sure invitation to burnout. It is crazy to think that people will always be thankful for what we do. And it is even crazier for us to think they will follow our advice.

I say this because people often have a sense of what friends and family should be like. They have rules of proper behavior and expect people in their lives to actually be this way. And when they aren't, they are frustrated, their blood pressure goes up and their self-esteem takes a dive. Instead, we need to look at the specific people, change our rules and enjoy who they can be. If they improve, lovely. If they don't, there should be no surprise.

Once a man came to see me and said that it was difficult for him to visit his parents. They never seemed to consider his feelings or believe what he was doing was worthwhile, and were terribly put out when he didn't respond to their every beck and call. He said, "They really get me angry. They just don't understand me."

"How old are they?" I asked.

"Mom is seventy-eight and Dad is eighty-six," he responded.

"Have they been this way your whole life?"

"Yes," he said.

"Well, maybe it is time to accept them as they are and not as you wish they were. If you are interested in doing this, you may have to let go of the fantasy that you will have a breakthrough with them. On the upside, you won't be let down and upset when you interact with them. What would you like to do? Would you like to take back the inordinate amount of power that you have given them or not?"

"At this stage, I just don't want them to have such an impact on me."

"All right, but you are going to think that what I am going to suggest is a bit strange. Are you willing to try it?"

"Sure. What is it?"

"The next time you visit them, when you pull your car up in front of the house, I want you to think you are visiting an insane asylum." Before he could say something, I quickly added, "Are you insulted by what I am suggesting?"

"No. Actually I feel that way sometimes when I get into such crazy discussions with them."

"It will help lower your expectations, so you won't go in feeling that they will respond to you as you think parents should. Ironically, if you feel free of the need for their approval and attention, they just might give it. But even if they do, still remember the image. Also, when talking on the phone with them, as soon as you hear their voices, think of what I said so that you won't expect them to respond as you wish them to. The reality is that while you would like them to behave in a particular way, they may not be able to do it."

He followed my wild suggestion, and with additional work on his "rules for how parents should treat their children," he was able to first resign himself and then ultimately accept the reality of who his parents were. Following this, he was then able to look for parental-type love as it is shown in little ways in so many other places in life, so that he could feel loved in healthy, encouraging relationships.

I often use humor, because one of the best ways to see how ridiculous our rules are is to be ridiculous in our approach. To take ourselves more lightly is essential for health—both psychological and spiritual. So, it is to this topic we shall now turn for some additional ideas on gaining and maintaining perspective in life.

. . . .

FOR REFLECTION...

What are your unspoken but powerful rules?

Have you taken the time to examine the "shoulds," "have tos," and "can'ts" in your life to see if they have to be this way? Also, what are the "fruits" of having such rules as these? Do they give you life and help you or do they hold you back?

Do you have a companion in life with whom you are comfortable enough to "think" aloud? Why is having such an intimate relationship important for spiritual and psychological health?

12. Taking Yourself Lightly

→

Avoiding overinvolvement with ourselves (extreme preoccupation with self) is very difficult. We don't want to lead the unreflective life. That makes sense. We need to take time out for introspection and self-awareness. That's also good. But it is so easy to become overinvolved in ourselves in the process.

That is why it is good to have friends to help us realize when we have lost our way. When I get moody, my wife, Michaele, will often say, "For goodness sake, call someone on the phone who really has a problem!" Naturally, I don't stand there and listen to such truths, but go off to profitably pout for a half hour or so. I think that pouting for a brief period of time is fine, as long as we don't do it too long. In the process of pouting, we can realize what ungrateful goofs we have been so that we can get on with the business of enjoying life. When the pouting continues, though, we need to come to the realization that we have lost perspective and should chat with a friend about it.

When we take ourselves lightly, we can even weather in a better way those little failures that come our way in life. Thinking of this reminds me of when I was up for a postdoctoral fellowship at Yale following my graduation from Hahnemann Medical College.

I was so excited about it. When I had called to see what my status was, they let me know that I was a finalist. I got so carried away with the news that in the evening, when I was taking my shower, I started singing "Boolah Boolah" to demonstrate my ability to sing "the essence" of Yale's school song.

When my wife heard me singing in the shower, she opened the door, put her head in the room and said, "Bob, don't work yourself up. You may not get in and then you will be crushed."

I said, "Do you realize that in this building you have the only finalist for a postdoc at Yale taking a shower in *your* bathroom? No one is going to take the joy away from me of being in this position, so please close the door so appropriate steam remains in the finalist's bathroom."

"All right," she said. "But don't say I didn't warn you."

Later that week, I called again when I hadn't heard from the people at Yale. There was an embarrassed silence on the other end of the phone when they realized who I was...followed by the infamous question, "Oh. Didn't you get a notice from us by mail as to our decision?"

When I heard that, I knew it was the "silver bullet" being shot into my hopes for attending Yale. They then informed me that one of the current postdocs decided to stay for another year, so the space for which I was applying would not be open.

I think that I took it well. I calmly got off the phone and immediately prayed that the fellow who decided to stay on would have his house infected with locusts.

After getting off the phone, I said to my wife, "This is terrible. What a rotten break! I didn't get in, and I had such high hopes about it based on my previous phone call to them."

She said, "Didn't I warn you about getting your hopes up?"

"Now please go easy," I said. "You don't step on a person when he's depressed. You cook him a nice meal. Offer to do what you can for him. That is the spiritual thing to do."

She looked at me with a wry smile and said, "You know, I think you even enjoy your depressions!" Then, even though I felt a bit bad and she felt sorry that I didn't get the position, we both laughed.

Taking ourselves lightly is essential in life today. We must laugh at ourselves and most things loudly and often so that when something important, *really* important, comes along, we have the energy and flexibility to take it seriously enough to act courageously instead of being overwhelmed.

There are a number of good rules to help us accomplish this. They include the following:

- Tease yourself more often during the day—especially when your feelings have been hurt. Too often, we give people the power to do what only we can do ourselves: people don't hurt us by their comments—we hurt ourselves by taking their statements to heart and forgetting the love of God for us as it is reflected in so many wonderful faces and experiences in our lives.

- Have healthy "harassers" in your life. These are the people who don't fall in line with our moodiness and exaggeration of things that really aren't important. In addition, they aren't put off by our anger. These persons help us eventually to see how much energy is wasted on being upset over little things. Too often today, we see everything done to us as symbolic of something larger. This waste of energy is limited by the healthy harassers in our lives.

- When upset, *always* question your assumptions underlying the reason for it. Being an administrator for much of my professional life, I often get letters of complaint. Some have merit; many are the result of perception and projection. For instance, once a student erroneously got dropped from a course. Rather than asking if this was in error, she wrote me a scathing letter. I wrote her back, informing her that it was a mistake that she

113

was dropped from the course. I added the prescription that the next time she wanted to send an angry letter before checking out the facts, she should go to her room, look in the mirror, make funny faces and tell herself to "lighten up and get a life!" (You should have seen the follow-up letter she sent me. I didn't know she knew so many bad words!)

– Discern what you can change and what you can't. There are so many things that are temporarily unchangeable. We need to continue to hope and pray about such things; however, we also need to do what we can about things on which we can make an impact. The well-known ecology phrase, "Think globally; act locally," is a good one to remember; otherwise, we will waste energy and become overwhelmed by always trying to tackle by ourselves those things that need a concerted effort. (Prayer of petition, by the way, is best defined as "making a concerted effort *with* God.")

The above rules and other ones that we can come up with (given our own different personality styles) are essential for the destruction of the negative grandiosity that often overwhelms us. As we learn to take God and spirituality more seriously, unfortunately we often take ourselves too seriously instead. I guess that is why I love and usually include in my books and lectures the warning of Charles Haddon Spurgeon to his fellow preachers. What he said to them certainly can be said to those of us in other occupations and professions as well:

> Some ministers would make good martyrs.
> They are so dry they would burn well.

Hopefully, we will do what we can to keep perspective so as not to be included among such human kindling wood because of the rigid ways we live out our lives.

. . . .

FOR REFLECTION...

What role does humor play in your life and relationships?

Why is it important to overlook many of the little annoyances and inconveniences of life?

When is the last time you laughed at your own foibles? How did it help you to maintain a healthy outlook on life?

13. Deep Gratefulness

→

Taking ourselves lightly allows us to recognize when we commit the mistake of *entitlement*. If we feel that life owes us more, we paradoxically wind up depriving life, ourselves and those whom we are called to guide (children, employees, students...). We fail to experience the spontaneous joy of reaping the benefits of what is already given to us. We live in a world filled with such very needy and demanding people. Such people, when faced with munificence, ignore it in order to inspect the overall situation to make sure that they are getting what they feel they deserve. The following popular story illustrates the type of person about whom I am speaking:

> A man would come in each day to a restaurant that served a small loaf of bread with its meals. Shortly after sitting down, he would ask for more bread to be served with his meal. After a few days of this, the waitress got tired of running back and forth, so she put two loaves of bread in front of him. Much to her surprise, he still finished them in record time and asked for more.
>
> She then gave him two baskets with four loaves when he came in next time— only to have him eventually demand more bread. Finally, she'd had it with him, so she talked to the baker prior to his next visit. The baker made a large loaf of bread

four feet by two feet in diameter. She thought to herself, "This will shut him up!"

When he came in and was seated, she went back to the kitchen for the bread. Struggling as she carried it to the table, but still smirking all the while she did it, she dropped it on the table in front of him. He looked at it, paused, looked up and said in a whiny voice, "Oh, so we're back to one piece of bread again, eh?"[15]

Sadly, we live in an age of neediness typified by this little story. As the well-known theologian Rabbi Abraham Heschel once noted:

"Every human being is a cluster of needs, some of which are indigenous to his nature, while others are induced by advertisement, fashion, envy, or come about as miscarriages of authentic needs....[Unfortunately] we usually fail to discern between authentic and artificial needs and, misjudging a whim for an aspiration, we are thrown into ugly tensions. Most obsessions are the perpetuation of such misjudgments. In fact, more people die in the epidemics of needs than in the epidemics of disease."[16]

There is also an Ojibwa saying that captures the dialectic of unnecessary neediness on the one hand, and the possibilities before us to embrace awe and true appreciation for life on the other. It states, "Sometimes I go about in pity for myself and all the while a great wind is carrying me across the sky." It is an image worthy of meditation.

Maybe we are fearful of being grateful. More people than I would care to count seem to be more comfortable complaining, searching and feeling more compatible with martyrdom than gratitude. More people than I dare estimate seem to be uncomfortable with carrying peace and joy in life. They are fearful of or uncomfortable with being grateful. To those of this ilk whom I encounter in therapy I give the task: "No matter how terrible you feel about it, no matter how very hard it is to do—I say, Go forth and enjoy life!"

For most of us, deep gratefulness—a natural sense of appreciation for breath, food, friends, good music, books, long leisurely walks and the other gifts of life, like good taste for the wonders of creation—must be cultivated. Our demanding society goes against this trend. Its messages are as follows: "You don't have enough!" "Be careful that you're not being cheated in some way of what you deserve!" (Such messages are certainly not like the Buddhist philosophy that helps us recognize that wanting less is certainly preferable to running through life seeking more.)

Yet, when we learn to taste gratitude and we can enjoy living fully with awe, our eyes will be opened to a new reality that will fill the part of our heart that feels so empty now. And, no matter how ungrateful and demanding we may feel at times, what more can we ask than this?

A Different Reality

Years back, my wife, daughter and I lived in a neighborhood that most people dream about today. We could leave the front door open. Neighbors were friends: not just acquaintances, but people who waved from their cars as they left for work in the morning and arrived at night.

So it was not reckless on my part to open the front door in the summertime when I woke up. Actually, it was a regular routine. I would get up early, put on the coffee, then open the back and front doors so that the breeze could work its way through the house, bringing with it the scent of the different flowering bushes and plants that flourished around the house.

However, one morning after I had brought our coffee upstairs and my wife and I were chatting for a bit while sitting in bed, I thought I heard a noise downstairs. When I went to the top of the stairs to listen for someone knocking at the screen door and yelling up at us to get out of bed and come down and serve them coffee, I heard what seemed to be the murmurs of little children.

When I went downstairs, sure enough, two children were sitting at our table having cereal as if nothing at all was unusual. When I walked in, they looked up and the older sister simply said, "My little brother was hungry and my parents are still sleeping, so we came over here for breakfast."

These two were hot stuff. They always had some little surprise in their conversations with us as well as in the pronouncements they occasionally made. One time, the younger brother came to the door and said to my wife, "Life is a blank and then you die!" Then in a stage whisper he added, "The word is not really 'blank,' but it's a bad word so I am not supposed to say it."

I always remembered this interaction because many people truly view life this way. Obviously, one or both of his parents did. We lose sight of the awe and wonder of the world so quickly. We even poison our children with our sense of life's stresses—without helping them see its daily promises.

Driving to the college where I teach, I would sometimes take advantage of an early start by stopping at my clinical practice en route. I didn't do this to check the mail or see a patient, but to walk through the pastures and woods of the retreat center in which I had my office. The paths stretched out for miles, and the surrounding fields were filled with deer and woodchucks, while the woods were home to birds and possum, squirrels and chipmunks that squeaked about my presence when they spied me.

Because the morning often would be wet, I would keep a pair of "wellies" in the back of my car so I could pull them on. With these green boots in place, I would stroll through the beautiful pastures and sometimes venture into the woods with a perennial smile on my face. It was heaven. It was peace.

When I eventually did get to work, I would sometimes mention my walks to others. Sometimes they would smile and launch into their own stories of long, leisurely walks or jogs through the woods, restful times sitting by a pond. Others talked about hiking up mountains where the air was so fresh that they felt moved by their feelings of freedom and relaxation.

However, just as often, a person would give me a look that would say, "Get real! You really do live with your head in the clouds." My mind would respond with the rhetorical question, "But which is real?" Is it the stress of daily competition or the peace of which we can avail ourselves every now and again by doing such things as walking in the country, sitting at a coffee bar or occasionally strolling down a sunny city street?

When people say to me "It must be nice!" when I relate one of my stories of getting away from it all so that I can regain or keep a perspective on life, I respond, "Yes. It is nice. Furthermore, it's free. It's available to anyone who wishes to walk there....It's all from God for the asking" (or more accurately, for the openness to perceiving it as gift).

Seeing reality with a sense of awe is based on the willingness to embrace a new perspective. Therefore, we must do all we can to seed such an attitude marked by gratitude—a deep gratitude that tells us even our daily life is a gift, a gift that we can easily ignore while we fantasize with desire about what is not in our lives. The shame of it is that when we are involved in this type of yearning and fantasizing, we miss so much that is in front of us and wind up feeling even more needy. The saying "To whom much is given, more will be added" is certainly apropos in this instance.

Feeling guilty or helpless about our inability to be grateful for what and who we are serves no good purpose, unless it wakes us up to the fact that we have a need for understanding the beauty that is already in our lives. Maybe we miss so much because no one educates us on how to fill our emptiness with awe and goodness. Maybe we just don't understand how to learn and teach each other how to "take in" all that is *already* in our schedule, environment and life. Maybe we need to learn how to see in a new way. Certainly such a course in perception would be well worth the effort.

. . . .

FOR REFLECTION...

How does gratitude for the goodness that surrounds you affect your relationships?

Are you able to recognize your own (occasional or persistent) selfishness or lack of gratitude? How might a healthy change in attitude and perspective alter these "stumbling blocks"?

Is it possible to be simultaneously grateful and selfish?

Think back to the "circle of grace" described at the close of chapter 1. How does deep gratefulness help us to keep the circle unbroken or intact?

14. Achieving a New Perspective: Seeing, REALLY Seeing

→

Perspective reveals what is before our eyes, including what we haven't been able to see because we didn't have the "vision" to experience what was there. Humorists show us this perspective by looking at the normal things of life, seeing what we see, but saying what never occurs to us to say because of the way we filter life while they embrace it with honesty and fun.

My favorite humorist, Erma Bombeck, was able to do this all of her life. The fact that she made a good living from it is no wonder, given her quips. For example, her observation about skiing: Never take up a sport that has an ambulance parked at the bottom of the hill. She saw things just as they are and was able to express herself to us in ways with which we could identify easily.

Perspective also helps us to see the strengths with which we have failed to credit ourselves. Too often, we are able to see our problems much more clearly than our talents, and that's a shame. It also causes us undue self-doubt.

Once a woman came in to see me and laid out a list of catastrophes that had happened to her. To the list she added a negative feeling that she had about herself. Furthermore, she felt that she was not very effective in dealing with these stresses.

I responded by saying, "Do me a favor. When we step outside

after the session, don't stand next to me if it looks like we're going to have a thunderstorm."

Laughingly, she recognized, maybe for the first time since the mishaps started, just how much she had been going through and she said: "Does it sound that bad?" I responded, "Yes. Quite obviously from my remark, it does. The first question I have is *not*, 'How have you failed to do the right thing when confronted by all these problems?' but 'How were you able to survive them all so well?'"

No matter what happens in our lives, it is very hard to maintain perspective and see what is *really* important in life. Perspective, a sense of gratitude for the people and gifts in our lives, and respect for the limits of life as well as the inevitability of death (*our* death as well as the deaths of our loved ones) need to be sought each and every day. Otherwise, they will fall by the wayside.

I have had people close to me suffer chronic pain for a number of years. I thought that the reminder of how tough life can be for these people gave me the right to let up on praying a bit each day to ensure that I remember to see life as pure gift. (I feel that prayer, more than anything else, helps me to center myself so that I can enjoy each dawn with spontaneous gratitude and not take anything for granted.) Then I went in for an ultrasound to see if a nodule I had was cancerous.

I must admit that there was something attractive about the old-time medicine, because almost everything was kept a secret from the patient. Not today, though. The consultant brought in a vivid color picture of the nodule that was taken during a previous endoscopy exam. He showed it to me and said that this is what we are worried about.

Thinking that I was being brave and direct, I said, "If it is cancerous, do you then schedule an operation to cut it out?" He said, "Oh no. Given the kind of tissue around it, we would have to cut out a whole section of your esophagus; you would lose thirty pounds and be out of work three months."

Trust me, after his comment, I was gifted then and there with immediate perspective for the next twenty-four hours!...and I went back to taking out some time each morning in silence and solitude to recall each day as gift. Prayer, once again, was not something to be cheated on. I recognized yet again how fleeting perspective is for me when I don't take time to reflect—and perspective is essential for a healthy spiritual and psychological life.

With perspective and gratitude, we are surrounded with gifts; we value "the now" so much because we don't know if tomorrow will come. When we have such an attitude, we find that what is already there before us which is good becomes more visible. When my oldest brother, Ron, had a cataract operation, he said that after they took off the bandages following the operation, he could see colors so much more clearly and vividly. When he reported this to the physician, the doctor told him that he had probably been losing his appreciation of color slowly as his eyes clouded over. I think that the same happens spiritually and psychologically as we move through life. Our spiritual acuity and gratefulness for the breath of life, the ability to swallow, walk, drink, smile and shake hands are lost. We forget to be grateful, to see life anew each day. When that happens, a "spiritual cataract" slowly develops and life dulls over; in response, we erroneously start to look for unique and "greater" gifts with a sense of disappointment and entitlement.

Sadly, in doing this, we set aside the gifts we already have enthusiastically and generously been given in life. Metaphorically, it is like receiving a gift from a wonderful, warm friend, only to discard and ignore it the next day while she looks on in sadness at our lack of appreciation. Sometimes, in my own simple theology, I wonder if God feels hurt when the gifts that we seem so happy to receive initially are so quickly dismissed as unimportant and dull.

Perspective also allows us to ask new questions of life. It enables us to look from the vantage point of being on a high mountaintop so that we can see sunsets and horizons spiritually and psychologically in such a way that our life changes and we can behave differently and live more peacefully and simply.

Once, during a presentation, a man asked the very overwhelming question: "Why is there so much evil in the world today?" After I affirmed that I could see why he asked this question and cited some of the terrible atrocities and abusive movements going on, I said that I had a question that I thought was even more puzzling. "Which is?" he asked. I replied, "Given the state of the world and our grasping, competitive, fearful, stressful nature, why is there still so much good in today's world?"

Perspective can allow little children in poor countries to play kick the can and laugh as they watch the rusted piece of tin jump from competitor to competitor. Simultaneously, a lack of perspective and gratitude may cause a rich tourist to complain if the bus is five minutes late. Instead of taking those moments of quiet to be at peace and filled with gratitude, the impatient tourist becomes so aggravated that he misses what is there to enjoy now in his life. The choices as to whether we live life joyfully and with appreciation are, in many cases, indeed up to us.

Don't Wait for the Next Train...
Being in "the Now"

I always loved the saying, "Life is something that happens while we are busy doing something else." The problem for us is that we always have a good reason to be in the future. We must plan, save, get ready. The problem is that while we are planning, we are missing life. While we are saving, we are spending the present without getting anything for it. While we are getting ready, we are losing the ability to enjoy *the now* when we get there; the only thing we will be trained for is to get ready for still another future.

One lawyer was telling me about his fear: that he would not have a significant relationship develop in the near future and that he would not be attractive enough to meet someone when he got older. He told me about all his efforts to ensure that he increased his chances to meet someone.

My response was that he was behaving like someone waiting for a train but never getting on. There was so much in his life that he wasn't enjoying because he was centering all his energy on a specific type of relationship. While he did this, his health, energy and beautiful personality were not being used advantageously; the museums, good friends, movies, good books, opportunities to go to concerts were all being bypassed. Oh, he would go to museums and concerts as well as visit good friends, but he could never be completely present to these moments because he was looking to the possibility of a certain kind of relationship in the future. His mind and hopes were elsewhere.

The irony was that since he was not filling himself up with the joy of the life he already had available to him, he was becoming more and more needy. This, in turn, would become evident to others, distance the healthy people around him and make him vulnerable to unhealthy relationships. Being in *the now* is very much tied to Jesus' phrase: "To whom much has been given, more will be added." The spiritual reality again: "If your eye is good, your whole body will be good (Mt 6:22)." Perceiving *the now* as gift can make all the difference in how we enjoy the present.

Being in *the now* is not merely paying attention during a peak experience. It is being aware in all settings, seeing the real food of what is to be learned and experienced—not the imaginary, menu food of a future fantasy.

Once, years ago, I went to a conference at Salve Regina College in Rhode Island. Magnificent. However, in my foolishness, when I arrived late, I had a number of martinis before going to bed. Needless to say, the gods of alcoholic justice (it felt like vengeance) woke me up at four in the morning with a blistering headache and the thought, "What a jerk you are!"

As I sat on the edge of my bed, I thought, "Well, Doctor, what are you going to do now? You can't sleep. You have a headache and no aspirin, and you feel like a bloody fool for drinking too much."

As silly and hypocritical as it seemed, I simply said, "Well, I always preach being in *the now,* so I may as well get up and be in it!!" So, as soon as the sun started to rise, I got up, put on my sweat-suit and went out toward the cliff trail to walk, not jog, along the water's edge. (Jogging made me feel that the top of my head would soon orbit around the sun, so I gave up that ridiculous idea.)

After walking for about twenty minutes, I noticed some kind of animal in the distance. I thought at first that it was a Pekinese dog or a large cat. However, when I got close, I realized that it was a beautiful fox. As I approached, I saw that there were actually three foxes...two adults and a little one curled under a bush.

After enjoying looking at them for a minute, I walked by, thinking how lucky I was to see them. After moving on about ten minutes more, I started to wish I had stayed longer. I had always marveled at the beauty and stealth of foxes and never had a chance to approach them so closely.

When I turned around to walk back, I was sure that they would be gone. But they were still there, so I sat on the rocks at a distance I felt they would be comfortable with and looked out over the water while I quietly prayed. The small fox stayed where he was, not paying me much attention. The adults on the rocks below just walked in circles for a few moments, like my Siberian husky dog used to do, and sat down as I had done. After a half hour together, I wished them good-bye, finished my prayers and moved on.

When I told the people at the conference later that day about my experience, they said that they would visit the trail tomorrow to try their luck. The next day it rained. It poured so hard that no one ventured outdoors. I was the only one from the conference who saw the foxes.

A headache is a poor excuse for being in *the now* as I was. But even though it's been a couple of years since I have had a drink—much less one of those martinis, which are strong enough to melt your face—I remember this episode.

The now is an amazing place that most of us rarely inhabit. While we spend our time in either nostalgia or the future, the present slips by. While we dream of acts of kindness, we fail to recognize that small actual works of joy in *the now* are what people remember. We may have said a few kind words to someone we met whose parent just died. Or, we may have teased a neighbor about a new car. These little things are the gifts that make their way into our hearts and change the day for the better or the worse. But being in *the now* also takes discipline and training to see what is of value in the open landscape of our lives. For, in the end, it is not stress that really takes the ultimate toll. It is the unusual problem of *acedia,* about which little is said directly today.

Facing Acedia

The horrors of addiction have finally come to light—not just addiction to alcohol, drugs and sex, but also to less obvious, normally considered good elements of life, such as work and health. Anything can lose its proper place in our life and become a compulsive activity. Spiritual leaders even warn us that this may be the case with respect to meditation, breakthrough experiences (what Zen *roshis* refer to as *kensho,* or prayer). Christian desert fathers and mothers, referred to as *Abbas* and *Ammas* during their fourth-century spiritual leadership in Persia and the north Africa wastelands, also warned us, "Seek God....Not where God lives." So we can even make the wonderful processes of reflection, prayer and discernment into "gods."

In seeking to uncover our addictions, asking the questions, "What preoccupies me in my life?" and "What or who is it in my life that is able to stir up most of my emotions of fear, anger, anxiety or stress?" are helpful. These questions will not only help us to discern what we are sensitive about, but will also direct us to what demands the heart of our attention. No matter what we may say about God from our faith perspective, knowing what preoccupies us or what is able to elicit the most dramatic emotional response tells us who our "god" really is.

However, what about *after* our addictions are ferreted out and addressed? What happens after we see what compulsive trends there are in our lives and we address them? Suppose, for instance, we have the welfare of our children as a compulsive activity. We recognize that we are worrying too much. We finally see that although being concerned about our children is good, we cannot control their lives or ensure their welfare, but can only do our best as role models and guides. Thus, having such an insight, we change our behavior, catch our fearful thinking and alter our view of the limits of ideal parenting so that we feel less anxious (and without us peering over their shoulders our children feel less anxious as well). Well, what then?

Some would expect that peace would arrive with the absence of worry. And they are right...*partially*. When we drop an addiction or remove a compulsion, immediate experiences of peace do occur, but they do not last. Instead, using the scriptural image of the room swept clean, other "demons" come and eventually fill the house more fully than before, if precautions are not taken. In other words, we find new worries, but this time we may seek more subtle ones that are less apt to be obvious to us (although it may be clear to our family and friends that we now have new causes or interests that have gotten out of hand).

So, the essential question after an addiction is removed is a new type of spiritual inquiry. It is this: "How will I live with the space that is now in my life?" Or, "Will I have the patience to allow myself to experience the emptiness or void in my life instead of leaping to fill it with something that may not be good food for the soul?"

Acedia, the "noontime demon" or "spiritual boredom" are the terms given to describe the experiences people have in today's stressful world when they give up an activity, fear, anxiety or compulsivity. Many problems faced today by therapists and spiritual mentors are the direct or indirect result of *acedia.*

Most people experience the edge of peace after they drop unnecessary defenses or addictions, but then become frightened by the openness. It is as if they wake up on a bright, sunny morning and they mentally go over and over their schedule until they come up with a list of troubles or activities they must face or do. We are trouble-making machines, and that is why psychologists, psychiatrists and counselors have been speaking about "symptom substitution" for years.

It is as if we feel the necessity to replace one difficulty with another. It is as if we fear being happy and at ease. It is as if we either don't deserve it or something bad will happen if we say that we are happy. But as one spiritual guide said to me when I was fretting a bit about not wanting to be caught unawares by just enjoying my presently happy life: "Don't be foolish. Life is hard enough in the real sense at times. Enjoy what is on your plate now and face the unpleasant food on your plate if and when it comes....Rejoice in *the now* so you will be grateful and strong; don't waste this time on the mountain."

How should we fill our lives? Well, in the following list of simple suggestions from my book, *After 50,* I think we can find some food for thought— some good food we can eat after we have eliminated the poisons of addictions and compulsions from our systems:

Nurturing a Hopeful Heart

Read a bit
Listen to a favorite song
Call a friend
Remember a kindness
Help the poor
Keep perspective
Smile broadly
Laugh loudly
Close doors gently
Do what you can
Live gratefully
Relax for a moment
Breathe deeply
Tease yourself often
Take a quiet walk
Tell God a funny story

So, with what I have suggested above and what you can add as wonderful supplements to the list, my only further suggestion about nourishing your soul is this: *enjoy!*

. . . .

FOR REFLECTION...

Think of someone you know who is able to see the humorous side of difficult or annoying situations. How does their "seeing" affect their own perspective in life as well as the perspectives of those in their company?

What does it mean to have a "hopeful heart"? Think of concrete ways of nurturing a hopeful heart in yourself; in others.

Deep Joy:
An Epilogue

→

Living a Gentle, Passionate Life has been about following simple journeys toward nourishing the human spirit and gathering what we can learn from them to keep perspective in our own lives. Clearly, one of the goals of this book has been to help us learn basic ways to "Keep our heads while those around us are losing theirs."

It is not difficult to feel the unease of people around us. Likewise, it is easy to see the negative feelings that people have about themselves and the future, and to experience the dark contagion of their feelings. However, I really do believe that it is not the amount of darkness in the world that will ultimately determine how we live. It is how we stand in this darkness that will matter.

The lure of social depression is certainly present today. Despair need not be the final word, however—no matter what has happened. I learned this when I visited Cambodia to work with the English-speaking helpers there. I was inspired by them; in addition, even though I was unable to speak to many Khmer people in the country, I was encouraged by their gentle, loving spirit.

When I was in Phnom Penh, I had a chance to walk around the city. As I got to the square down by the Mekong River, I took a few pictures and then stood back, taking in the scene. From the corner of my eye I could see a woman walking toward me with her belongings perched upon her head. I didn't want to stare, but I did glance in her direction to see how she was keeping it all balanced on her head, since I have trouble keeping a hat on mine.

She looked toward me, smiled and said, "Hello." I was so surprised by this warm greeting, knowing as I did how much the people had been through in this country and how burdened by it all they must have been. I couldn't even respond.

She wasn't fazed a bit. She gave me a look, nodded as if to say, "Yes, you!" and repeated her comment, "Hello." This second greeting broke my trance, and I mumbled, "Oh, hello." In response, she just laughed lightly and walked by.

Later that morning, when I was halfway back to where I was staying, it started to rain heavily, turning the dusty streets into gluey rivulets of mud. I looked for a sheltered spot to stand until the worst of it passed. I saw an awning by a shop and ducked under the edge of it. There was also another customer there, sitting on a little table. He looked at me, smiled and pointed to another spot on the table. As I took my spot, he seemed very gratified that I would share his little place of rest and shelter from the quick-moving storm.

These two brief interactions happened in a country darkened by torture, killing and the persistent danger of land mines (when it rains, they float into previously considered safe areas to set the stage for farmers to be maimed and killed). My appreciation of these brief moments with people whose gratitude for the little things in their lives allowed them to be both joyful and friendly is in no way meant to belittle, gloss over, avoid, deny or be naive about the terrors that people must endure. Similarly, I do not mean to hide the hurts, poverty, unemployment, racism, abuse, hunger and violence that we encounter in our own lives. But these two passing meetings with people with whom I could not even converse remind me to challenge the uncritical acceptance of what society sells us every day as the common sense of natural despair. It is what I refer to today as "social depression."

For too long, the attitude has been either "Why bother? Just get what you can for yourself," or "The problems are too big; the responses you can make would be too insignificant." However, big problems aren't usually cured by large, once-and-for-all solutions. As a matter of fact, dramatic efforts to cure often wind up killing the patient. Contrary to this pervasive view, we need to see the value in a series of little responses, once we have discerned what we can do and what we are being called to do.

Society today likes to emphasize negativity and looks with a jaded view upon anyone who tries to make a positive impact. The media's favorite gambit is to try to find saints and then show that they have clay feet. For instance, one of the finest contemporary writers I know today wrote a book about famous people. In it he included Mother Teresa and then proceeded to vilify her.

When I heard about his writings, I was saddened—not because Mother Teresa was perfect in her life—no one is, and certainly she wasn't. However, while this man, like me, sat in his lovely home in a first-world country, she devoted her life kneeling beside dying and starving people, holding up their bodies and spirits.

Dorothy Day was once told by someone in the press that she was being referred to as a saint. She said (and I am liberally paraphrasing), "Oh no, I'm not going to let them get away with making me into a saint so they don't have to look at themselves and what they should be doing to help the poor."

We need to see what we can do for others in life if we are to have joy within us. For it is in living lives open to others that we find our own true selves.

Sartre said, "One must choose to live or to narrate." It is the people who actually initiate good actions that will feel something within themselves when they give. Hiding won't suffice, though it may give an illusion of security. Ignorance is no excuse either.

Deep Joy: An Epilogue

The philosopher Karl Popper had an interesting insight about people claiming they didn't know about the holocaust: they weren't ignorant— they just didn't want to know.

We must act. We must risk. We must recognize that courage will catch up with us if we continue to walk ahead. As I advise my patients, "Don't panic...instead, keep moving."

But if caring actions and compassion represent one leg of living a gentle, passionate life, then our own sense of spirituality is the other. We need both to make up the "circle of grace" I alluded to earlier.

As I pointed out, when the circle is broken, our spirituality may become so narrowly pietistical, our God so small, that we will be praying to ourselves. And when the circle is broken, compassion runs the risk of changing for the worse as well. Rather than being a natural outgrowth of love that opens our eyes to see life and God anew, compassion will turn into just another form of compulsive giving that will bring down everyone in the process.

So, as was pointed out earlier, we need a spirituality— an openness to a wonderful relationship with the truth about ourselves, others and God— that is not just a vague urge to feel more at peace. We need an attitude of single-heartedness that is joined with a real sense of identity that is not based on others' views, but on a deep belief in our own unique value. When we have single-heartedness, identity and compassion as our guides, then an attitude of greater simplicity and continued spiritual progress becomes possible. We can be in a spiritual and psychological place in which we appreciate our "ordinary" self rather than being overcome by our previously scattered nature or the fantasy that we need to do something spectacular to overcome our sense of stagnation.

We will have direction, and our quiet time will be like the lights of a car that shine upon where we need to move next in the darkness. We will simply put one foot in front of the other, knowing that we are not drifting or being driven, but are actually flowing with life...a gentle, passionate life marked by deep joy.

This book about "country psychology" and spirituality, then, has been about simple possibilities. It has tried to offer some basic ideas, stories and principles designed to show how we can nourish the human spirit— ours and that of those whom we meet each day. In truth, nothing radical has been shared; nothing really new has been revealed. In fact, though, what I have tried to do is to dust off basic spiritual and psychological truths as reminders that need to be brought to the fore again if we are to live with a sense of hope and commitment.

The world needs such good energy today, as it always has in the past. You and I are the ones who must provide it. If we, the people who say we value a meaningful life, don't do it, then who will? Certainly, we must try...for it is in the circle of grace— of spirituality and compassion—where we will find the real life that we seek.

Notes

→

1. Henri Nouwen addresses these questions, but from a slightly different vantage point in his beautiful little book *Making All Things New* (San Francisco: Harper and Row, 1981).

2. Quoted in Henri Nouwen's *Genesee Diary* (New York: Doubleday, 1976), p.107. He attributes the source to a statement made in an interview with William Sloane Coffin.

3. Robert F. Rodman, *Keeping Hope Alive: On Becoming a Psychotherapist* (New York: Harper and Row, 1986), p. 5.

4. Quoted in Thomas Merton, *A Vow of Conversation* (New York: Farrar, Straus & Giroux, 1988), p. 10.

5. Anthony Storr, *Solitude: A Return to the Self* (New York: Ballantine Books, 1988), p. 18.

6. *Ibid.*, p. 35.

7. *Ibid.*, p. 36.

8. Andrew Harvey, *A Journey to Ladakh* (Boston: Houghton-Mifflin, 1983), p. 65.

9. I am grateful to Diane Capozzi for sharing this story with me.

10. This beautiful story is told by Bill McIntyre, M.M., who knew and worked with Mother Teresa.

11. Citation for this Merton quote unknown.

12. Kathleen Norris, *Dakota* (Boston: Houghton-Mifflin, 1993), p. 38.

13. Unfortunately, I do not know the exact source for this quotation.

14. Quoted in Thomas Merton's *A Vow of Conversation,* p. 20.

15. I am thankful to Jeff Dauses for having first introduced me to this popular story.

16. Abraham Joshua Heschel, *Man Is Not Alone* (New York: Farrar, Straus & Giroux, 1972), p. 182.